HAS THIS HAPPENED TO YOU?

1. You're stuck in traffic and your yellow "check engine" light comes on. Do you need to pull over to the side and call for the tow truck? *(no)* Should you just continue to your destination and take your car to the shop later? *(yes)* Can you safely just ignore the whole episode? *(no)*

2. There's an odor of burning plastic in the car. Is it the electrical system? *(not likely)* The brakes? *(could be)* Or has a dry cleaner's bag stuck to the exhaust? *(best bet)*

3. Your car refuses to start and you hear a grinding sound when you turn on the ignition. Should you give up and call the tow truck? *(not right away)* Can you get the car to start using some of Bob's helpful hints? *(probably)* If you get it started, will the problem recur? *(definitely—take it to the garage to replace the starter drive or the starter)*

Don't be left stranded, compromise your safety, or break the bank on unnecessary car repairs. Bob Cerullo can save you time, money, and headaches by helping you find out—

WHAT'S WRONG WITH MY CAR?

BOB CERULLO is a certified Master Mechanic with his own 23-bay auto repair shop. He's a regular contributor to *Motor Magazine* and *Parade*, he hosted "The Auto Show," a popular weekly call-in program for people with car trouble on WOR radio in New York, and millions have seen him on "Late Night with David Letterman." Bob Cerullo lives in New York City.

What's Wrong with My Car?

BOB CERULLO

Ⓟ

A PLUME BOOK

PLUME
Published by the Penguin Group
Penguin Books USA Inc., 375 Hudson Street,
New York, New York 10014, U.S.A.
Penguin Books Ltd, 27 Wrights Lane, London W8 5TZ, England
Penguin Books Australia Ltd, Ringwood, Victoria, Australia
Penguin Books Canada Ltd, 10 Alcorn Avenue,
Toronto, Ontario, Canada M4V 3B2
Penguin Books (N.Z.) Ltd, 182–190 Wairau Road,
Auckland 10, New Zealand

Penguin Books Ltd, Registered Offices:
Harmondsworth, Middlesex, England

First published by Plume, an imprint of Dutton Signet,
a division of Penguin Books USA Inc.

First Printing, September, 1993
10 9 8 7 6 5

Adaptations of three sections, "Ten Questions for Your Mechanic," "Caring for
Your Car Is Your Responsibility," and "How to Save Money Caring for Your
Car," originally appeared in *Parade* magazine.

 REGISTERED TRADEMARK—MARCA REGISTRADA

LIBRARY OF CONGRESS CATALOGING-IN-PUBLICATION DATA:
Cerullo, Bob.
    What's wrong with my car? / Bob Cerullo.
       p.   cm.
    ISBN 0-452-26993-8
    1. Automobiles—Maintenance and repair.   2. Automobiles—Defects.
    3. Automobiles—Performance.   I. Title.
    TL152.C43   1993
    629.28′72—dc20   93-16986
                                                                        CIP

Printed in the United States of America

BOOKS ARE AVAILABLE AT QUANTITY DISCOUNTS WHEN USED
TO PROMOTE PRODUCTS OR SERVICES. FOR INFORMATION
PLEASE WRITE TO PREMIUM MARKETING DIVISION, PENGUIN
BOOKS USA INC., 375 HUDSON STREET, NEW YORK, NEW YORK
10014.

This book is dedicated to
Vincent J. Cerullo, Sr.
Master Mechanic
my father, my mentor,
and my very good friend

CONTENTS

SYMPTOMS

Section I.   Starting the Car

Section II.   Steering

Section III.   Brakes

Section IV.   Warning Lights

Section V.   Sounds, Smells, Smoke, and Leaks

Section VI.   Miscellaneous Malfunctions

APPENDIXES

A. Safety Tips, Emergency Repair, and Basic Car Care

B. Know More About Your Car

ACKNOWLEDGMENTS

I would like to thank my father, Vincent J. Cerullo, Sr., who taught me the trade; my mother, Gertrude Young Cerullo, who encouraged me to write, my wife, Marilynn Mannix Cerullo, whose understanding, encouragement, and support made it all possible; my children, Tara, Merry, and Robert, for their inspiring support and contributions; Mr. J. Robert Connor, who first gave me the opportunity to write for *Motor* magazine; Mr. Kenneth Zino, who gave me the opportunity to write my first monthly column "Trade Secrets"; Ms. Gael McCarthy for encouraging me to write for *Parade* magazine; Mr. Herb Shuldiner, who first asked me to write for *Popular Science* magazine; Mr. Richard Taylor, who gave me my first exposure to talk radio; Ms. Kathy Novak, whose support motivated me to get involved in talk radio; Mr. Maurice Tunik, who first hired me to co-host a talk radio automotive show on the ABC radio network; Mr. Bob Bruno, who hired me to develop the "Auto Show" on WOR radio; Mr. Jerry Carroll, who taught me how to talk on the radio; Ms. Michelle Marbury, who taught me how to conduct a talk-radio program; Ken and Daria Dolan, who first introduced me to television; David Letterman, who nicknamed me "The Car Guy" and gave me national exposure on his "Late Night" program; Ms. Kim Kennedy, for teaching me about TV; Mr. Joe Franklin, for his support and friendship; Ms. Audrey LaFehr, who came up with the idea for this book; and finally, all those good people who have, over the years, telephoned their car questions to me on radio and TV.

Introduction

Long before I could actually see over the dashboard of my father's car, I had already put in countless hours behind the wheel make-believe driving—when I could finally reach the pedals of a big tow truck my father owned. That is, until one afternoon when I accidentally started the truck. My make-believe driving became real driving as the truck roared to life and I steered it through a busy intersection and down the street, where I eventually parked it, hoping my dad would not realize I was the one who had moved the truck. Of course, he immediately discovered who the driver had been, but he never reprimanded me. The next day he started giving me driving lessons, despite the fact that I was several years away from getting a license. The narrow seventy-five-foot driveway next to our home became my highway. The confined space of my father's large auto-repair shop became my obstacle course. By the time I was ready to be tested for my driver's license, I was probably a better driver than the driving instructor, and I unquestionably knew more about how cars work and how they are repaired. I was fortunate to have gained this knowledge very early and pretty much as part of my youthful learning process. I wish every driver could have this type of learning experience.

My point is that for a majority of new drivers, learning to drive is complicated by learning how the car works, from the point of view of what happens when you step on the brake or turn the steering wheel. Learning about what makes the car move, steer, and stop is generally left to chance simply because it isn't really required knowledge for obtaining a driver's license in this country. The longer anyone drives, the more they are likely to know about how their car works. Over a period of time they will accumulate experience that will enhance their knowledge. For those who are interested in cars, that experience may be broadened by reading various books about the basics of how a car works. There are any number of books available that will explain the fundamental concepts of what propels, steers, and stops a car. In my experience, those people who have taken the time to read about how their car works or have taken a basic course in auto-repair fundamentals are generally far more confident owning and driving a car than are those people who never take their driver education beyond obtaining a license. Many who know nearly nothing about how a car works or what happens when a problem develops are actually afraid of what will happen to them every time they get behind the wheel. In local city driving they are simply apprehensive. Out on a major highway they are truly afraid. At night on a deserted country road they are gripped with terror. I have had callers to my radio programs ask me if a certain sound means the car is going to blow up. I know of dozens of car owners who have been ripped off by unscrupulous mechanics who prey on a car owners' unjustified fears of a particular noise or odor.

The idea for this book came as a result of my weekly talk-radio programs on the ABC network and later on WOR Radio 710 in the New York metropolitan area. In those years I answered literally thousands of calls from car owners who were frightened, intimidated, concerned, frustrated, and even victimized by owning a car. I have tried to offer in the following pages the information my listeners frequently asked for on the radio shows, and have tried to cover the concerns I have talked about on numerous television programs and written about in magazines. This book will provide you with a ready reference source so that you can quickly understand what is happening to your car when you suddenly discover an unfamiliar noise, odor, condition, or circumstance you have never experienced before while driving. When you know what is wrong, you can make a reasonable assessment of what you need do to safely resolve a problem.

This book is intended to inform you about what is wrong. Although it does include tips and simple solutions, it is not intended to turn you into an automobile mechanic. However, I am sure that as you go along you will accumulate an understanding of your car, and this will make your dealings with your auto mechanic less of a chore. It will help eliminate much of the mystery that goes into having your car repaired, a mystery that comes about when you cannot clearly communicate a problem to your mechanic. When you know what needs to be done, you become less suspicious of the honest mechanic who is doing the right thing to repair your car.

Every car will need to be repaired at some point. Getting your car repaired need not be a traumatic experience. I caution you to use this book as an aid to your understanding. Diagnosing your own problems can be costly and dangerous. You should use this book to better understand the source of the problem and to help you explain it so that your mechanic can save time by going directly to the source. When you encounter an unfamiliar condition, refer to the first section and try to match the symptoms found there as closely as possible with what is happening to you. Don't jump to conclusions after the first set of symptoms that seem to match. Read about similar symptoms and come back to the one you feel most closely corresponds to your problem. Remember that there are differences between one car and another. It would be impossible to list every condition for each of the more than six hundred models of cars available in this country. What I have tried to do is list the most common conditions and what is happening when they occur.

I urge you, when time permits, to refer to the second part of the book to further develop your understanding of the parts of your car associated with a particular problem. If, for example, the symptoms point to a brake problem, use the opportunity to develop a better understanding of your car's braking system. Ask your mechanic to show you the parts and explain what he is doing to repair the problem. If your problem is difficult steering, go beyond the first section and learn how your car steers.

I know from my years of experience diagnosing and repairing car problems that the more you know about your car, the more fun it is to own and drive. Who knows? You might even become a car enthusiast and eventually take great pleasure in owning and repairing your own fleet of cars. You would be amazed how many very wealthy people, who have absolutely no need to save money repairing their own cars, take great pleasure in doing most of their own repair work on new and old cars they have collected. You might not want to take your understanding that far, but you would certainly enjoy knowing precisely what your mechanic is talking about when he tells you it is going to cost several hundred dollars to repair a problem. When you hear a new sound coming from the brakes or when you feel the steering wheel momentarily stiffen on a turn, it should mean something to you. You can save literally hundreds of dollars and perhaps prevent a dangerous accident if you are tuned in to the sounds, sights, smells, and feel of your car.

This book is intended to make you comfortable driving your car, to make you more at ease with your car through a better understanding of what is going on when your car does something different. You will be a safer, smarter, and wiser driver when you can answer the question, *What's wrong with my car?*

Starting the Car

Ignition Key Won't Turn

Symptoms

You parked the car and did some shopping; then, when you returned to the car, you found you couldn't turn the ignition key.

Explanation

For an ignition lock to work properly, the key must actually push a series of pins into the correct position. Over time, the pins become dry and do not move easily. This causes wear on the key and can eventually cause the lock to malfunction. It is a good idea, even on a new car, to lubricate the ignition-lock cylinder, the door locks, and the trunk-lock cylinder with WD-40 or an equivalent lubricant when you do your oil change.

Diagnoses and Solutions

One: First, make sure you have the correct key for the ignition. Next, grasp the steering wheel with your left hand and the ignition key with your right hand. Pull down on the steering wheel as if you were steering to the left as you try to turn the ignition key. If that doesn't work, try pushing up on the wheel as if you were turning to the right, while at the same time turning the ignition key. Very often this problem occurs because you have turned the wheels too far either to the right or left when you were parking. This in itself is not a bad idea, in that it is more difficult to steal a car whose wheels are turned all the way to one side.

Two: Examine the ignition key carefully. A worn or bent ignition key might not work. If you have another set of keys, try turning the ignition with a different key. If the other key works, discard the worn key. Don't make a duplicate key from the worn key; you will have the same problem. If the key is just bent, you might be able to straighten it by gently squeezing it in the jaws of a vice.

Three: Ignition locks can eventually wear. If you find the lock is difficult to turn or will not turn at all, try spraying WD-40 lubricating fluid into the lock cylinder. WD-40 is available at most hardware stores, supermarkets, and auto-supply stores. Spray some on the key, too. Then try working the key slowly to free the lock cylinder. Consider replacing the ignition-lock cylinder as soon as possible.

No Start/No Sound

Symptoms

You turn the ignition key to the start position and you hear no sound at all.

Explanation

Once an engine is started, the alternator must constantly recharge the battery. If an alternator belt breaks, this recharging isn't done. If a booster battery succeeds in starting the engine and you're sure you didn't leave the lights on, it is important to have the charging system checked, the battery tested, and to make sure there are no electrical drains. A drain could be caused by a malfunctioning trunk or glove-compartment light that stays on after the trunk or glove-compartment door is closed.

Diagnoses and Solutions

One: Check the shift selector to be sure it is in park or neutral.

Two: Check the headlight switch. If you find it already turned on, you have probably discharged the battery and will need a booster battery to jump-start the dead battery. Also check the interior light switch. Interior lights, if left on long enough, can also discharge the battery.

Three: Turn on the headlight switch. Get out of the car and look at the headlights. No headlights or a dim, orange-colored light means a partially discharged battery. You will need a booster battery. Two bright headlights mean a starter or switch problem, for which you need to see a mechanic.

Four: If there are no headlights with the headlight switch on, the battery terminals connecting the battery cables to the battery might be loose or dirty. Be sure to turn off the headlights before you attempt to clean or tighten battery terminals. If the headlights come on after cleaning the terminals, try starting the car again.

> **CAUTION:** Sparks near a battery can cause it to explode. See page 194 for the proper way to boost a dead battery.

No Start/Clicking Sound

Symptoms

You turn the ignition switch to the start position and hear a rapid clicking or ratcheting sound from the engine.

Explanation

Either the battery is discharged (dead) or is not able to transmit its energy. An accumulation of crusty white powder on the terminals where the wires attach to the battery can cause resistance to the flow of current. Also, a solenoid switch in the starter will often jam up when you try to start a discharged battery.

Diagnoses and Solutions

One: Wait a few minutes and try again. The battery is discharged, but there might be just enough electrical power left to crank the engine and allow it to start. Do not frantically pump the gas pedal. All this will do is flood the engine with gasoline and keep it from starting.

Two: If the engine still doesn't start after three or four tries, check for corroded battery terminals. Use water to flush the crust away. A garden hose is best if available. Then remove the terminals by loosening the clamp bolts. Steel wool or a special battery-cleaning brush should be used to clean the surface of the battery terminal and the cable clamp.

Three: If you've cleaned the terminals and the engine still won't start, then a booster battery will be needed. Follow the booster procedure on page 194. Once the engine has started, allow it to run thirty minutes or longer to allow your car's own 12-volt alternator time to recharge the battery, or have the battery recharged at a service station.

Four: If you hear the clicking sound and then suddenly no sound at all, you might have to tap the starter. A jammed starter will prevent a fully charged booster battery from starting the car. You might be able to get the starter to work by tapping it with a hammer. Tap the body of the starter with the hammer several times, then try again to start the engine. Don't try this unless you're familiar with the location and appearance of the starter motor.

CAUTION: Refer to page 194 for the proper procedure for boosting a dead battery. If you tap the starter with a hammer, be sure the ignition switch is off, the shift selector is in park, and the parking brake is set. Also read page 255.

No Start/Grinding Sound

Symptoms

You turn the ignition switch to the start position and you hear a grinding sound, as if the teeth of two gears were grinding against each other. There might also be a loud banging sound or bell sound as the grinding sound stops.

Explanation

The grinding noise you hear is the starter drive gear trying to mesh with the engine flywheel gear. If the two gears do not mesh, they can't start the car, and are probably damaging each other. Waiting twenty minutes may allow the starter drive to engage the flywheel gear. This could save you a tow, but it is not a repair. The starter drive will probably grind the next time you try to start. The problem needs mechanical repair.

Diagnoses and Solutions

One: Turn the ignition switch to the start position. If the grinding persists, turn off the switch and wait two minutes. Try again, but do not keep the ignition switch in the start position when you hear the grinding. Try several times, but never allow the grind to continue. If the starter finally engages, do not shut the engine off until you get to a mechanic or find backup transportation. It might not restart.

If the car has not started, wait about twenty minutes and try again. If the engine doesn't start after a few tries, wait two or three hours before attempting to restart. If you still don't have success, let the car sit overnight. If it doesn't start in the morning, it's not going to, and you need to have the car towed to a mechanic. If your car has a standard transmission, you may be able to push the car to start (see page 14).

CAUTION: Repeated attempts to start when you hear the grinding could result in costly damage to the flywheel gear and the starter. If you experience a grind before the engine starts, do not dismiss it as just another new sound. The grind is a symptom of a worn starter drive or defective starter. The starter drive or complete starter will have to be replaced to repair the problem. Repair this problem as soon as possible. Delay could cause costly flywheel damage.

No Start/Spinning Sound from Starter

Symptoms

You turn the ignition switch to the start position, and instead of the normal cranking sound, you hear a spinning sound, or hear the starter first engage, then change to the spinning sound.

Explanation

When you turn the ignition switch to the start position the starter motor shaft starts to turn. As it picks up speed, a gear attached to the starter motor shaft called the *starter drive* must engage the flywheel gear which is attached to the engine crankshaft. When the starter drive gear does not engage the flywheel gear, the sound you hear is the rapidly spinning starter motor shaft. What you do not hear is the sound of the engine being turned over by the starter motor. It is a different kind of a sound than what you will hear when the starter motor drive gear and the flywheel gear mesh together normally.

Diagnoses and Solutions

One: Allow the motor to come to a complete rest. This takes more time than you might expect. To be sure, wait two minutes before you retry starting. If you again hear the spinning sound, release the ignition key. Do not pump the gas pedal before each start. This can cause the engine to flood with gasoline and not start.

Two: Do not retry starting for about two hours. Then follow the procedure described in solution One.

Three: If waiting two hours doesn't help, a longer period

of time might do so. Leave the engine overnight without trying to start. The next morning, follow the procedure described under solution One. If the car still does not start, you will need a tow truck for a car with an automatic transmission. If you have a standard transmission, you should be able to push-start the car. If you attempt to push-start a car with a standard transmission, you should first make sure the bumpers of the two cars are the same height. If they are not, you may cause expensive body damage or break your taillights or the headlights on the car doing the pushing. When push-starting, you must have the ignition key on and the transmission car in gear. Depress the clutch until the car is rolling, then slowly let it out. This will cause the engine to crank and it should start. When it does start, you can expect a sudden surge of power. Be ready to control the gas and the brakes when the engine suddenly starts. Small cars can also often be pushed by a couple of people.

CAUTION: Do not allow the starter to spin freely for any longer than it takes for you to release the key.

Engine Starts, Then Stalls

Symptoms

You start the engine in the normal way, but when you shift into gear, it stalls.

Explanation

When an engine is started, particularly on a cold day, there are additional systems that must operate to keep the engine running until it has had time to warm up. Gasoline does not vaporize well when it is cold, so carburetor-equipped engines have an automatic choke and a device known as a *fast idle* to keep the engine from stalling cold. Fuel-injected engines accomplish this using electronic sensors and electronic idle-speed controls. These systems are often related to what is generally known as a stalling problem. There are several other reasons an engine may stall, including the need for a carburetor base-idle adjustment or a tune up. Simply speaking, shifting the engine from neutral to drive adds the extra burden on the engine of turning the transmission torque converter. If the engine is idling too slowly, stalling may occur when you release the gas pedal or shift into gear. Also see pages 235, 239.

Diagnoses and Solutions

One: Start the engine as you normally would, but wait for at least ten minutes before shifting it into gear. If the engine then runs normally and does not stall, drive it as you would normally. If it stalls again the next time you start the car, have your mechanic check the choke and fast-idle system on a carbureted engine. It might need only a cleaning or an adjustment. For cars with fuel-injection systems, the diagnosis is more complicated. It might require that your mechanic test for a problem in the cold-enrichment system of the fuel injection.

Two: Start the engine as you normally would, but this time keep your left foot pressed firmly on the brake; operate the gas pedal with your right foot. Press down slightly on the gas pedal to keep the engine running faster as you shift into gear. You can expect the transmission to jump into gear, so be sure your left foot is pressed firmly on the brake. When you come to a traffic light, you will have to keep the car from lurching ahead by pressing firmly on the brake. Keep just enough pressure on the gas pedal with your right foot to prevent the engine from stalling. Drive slowly to the nearest mechanic. Use this two-foot driving technique only in an emergency situation. Before you attempt two-foot driving, read the following caution.

> **CAUTION: Two-foot driving as previously described should be attempted only in an emergency. It is very easy to become confused while driving with two feet and accidentally press the gas pedal instead of the brake pedal. This could cause you to lose control of the car. A good way to learn how to drive with two feet in an emergency is to practice in a large empty parking lot early on a Saturday or Sunday morning when you are sure there are no other people around. Don't try two-foot driving in traffic unless you are confident that you are fully in control.**

Normal Starter Sound but No Start

Symptoms

You turn the ignition key to the start position. The starter begins cranking the engine normally but the engine does not start.

Explanation

When an engine turns over normally, you hear first the sound of the starter cranking the engine, then, as the engine starts, the sound changes to something more like a roar. When the starter works normally but the engine does not roar to life, you know two things for sure: the battery is working properly and so is the starter. You do know that it is very likely that either the fuel-to-air mixture is at fault, or there is a poor spark (or even none) at the spark plugs. There certainly are many other possible causes, not the least of which is a broken timing belt (see page 247) or a worn-out engine.

Diagnoses and Solutions

One: Turn the ignition switch to the start position, then check the fuel gauge. You might be simply out of gas.

Two: If you depress the gas pedal several times before starting an engine with a carburetor, it is quite possible that you have flooded the engine. Flooding simply means that too much gasoline has mixed with the air to allow the mixture to ignite. Press the gas pedal to the floor to open the choke. Most carburetors are designed so that pressing the pedal to the floor and keeping it there opens the choke to clear the flood of gasoline. Crank the engine. You should feel the engine try to start. Allow the starter to turn to clear the mixture of fuel and air. Do not keep trying short bursts of the starting operation. Keep your foot down on the gas pedal until you hear the engine start to run. As the engine speed (rpms) increases, release pressure on the gas pedal. On some fuel-injected engines the flood-clearing process is automatic. Read your owner's manual to determine the correct procedure for starting your fuel-injected engine.

Three: You will nearly always find the carburetor in the center of the engine under the large, round air-filter assembly. On most cars, you simply unscrew the wing nut at the top center of the air filter, which allows you to lift the assembly off the carburetor. On top of the carburetor there is a flat plate called the choke. It must be closed over the carburetor opening for a cold engine to start. You must touch the accelerator pedal to release the choke to permit it to close on a cold engine. If the choke does not close automatically, try gently pushing it closed by hand after you have released the choke through one of two methods: step on the gas pedal or pull on the gas-pedal linkage. The gas-pedal linkage connects the carburetor to the gas pedal. It is generally a quarter-inch-diameter rod or cable attached to the side of the carburetor. The choke valve should now snap into the closed position. Replace the air-filter assembly and try starting the car. On fuel-injected engines there is no choke valve to close. Your only hope is to try pumping the gas pedal several times.

Four: Carburetor engines have an accelerating pump that will provide extra fuel for a cold start when the choke won't close. If you are sure the choke isn't closing, try depressing the gas pedal several times. Then try starting.

CAUTION: Whenever you remove the air filter and try to start the engine, you increase the risk of being injured should there be a backfire. Always reinstall the air filter before you attempt to start. Stand well clear of the engine before you give the signal for anyone to try starting. *Never* pour gasoline directly into the carburetor.

No Start, with Warm Engine and Normal Starter Sound

Symptoms

You turn the ignition key to the start position and the starter engages but the engine will not start.

Explanation

On a warm engine, when the starter cranks the engine normally but the engine will not start, the problem is most often related to a too rich fuel mixture caused by a carburetor or fuel-injection problem. Worn spark plugs or other defects in the ignition system may also interrupt the starting process. While you cannot assume any one thing is the cause of all warm-engine starting problems, it is likely they are fuel-related. You need fuel and ignition delivered at a precise moment for the engine to start and run: If electrical current is not being delivered to the ignition system, the engine will not start. If the fuel does not get delivered to the cylinders, either by the fuel injectors or the carburetor, the engine will not start. And if the timing belt or timing chain—or even a timing adjustment—is defective the engine will not start (also see page 239).

Diagnoses and Solutions

One: Press the gas pedal to the floor and turn the ignition key to the start position to crank the engine. Try cranking the engine for a minute or two. This should clear a flood on most carbureted engines. On fuel-injected engines, do not depress the gas pedal. Check the owner's manual for the correct starting procedure. Allow the engine to cool for a few hours, if possible, and try to restart.

Two: If solution One does not help, it is time to call for a tow truck. If you are stranded with no help available, you might want to try to determine why the car won't start. Check to see if the spark plugs are getting the electrical current they need to create a spark. First remove one of the spark-plug wires from the spark plug. Don't just grasp the wire and yank it off; grasp the thick rubber boot at the spark plug and twist it as you pull it off. Next, stick a screwdriver or even your oil dipstick into the end of the wire where it snapped onto the spark plug. Do not hold the metal part. (See the following Caution.) If possible, use an insulated plier or something that will not conduct high voltage. A wooden stick will do in an emergency. Arrange the screwdriver or dipstick so that it is a quarter of an inch away from a solid metal part of the engine. Have a friend crank the engine. If you're alone, try to reach in to the ignition switch with your right hand and look at the end of the spark-plug wire you disconnected as you crank the engine. There should be a bright blue spark in the quarter-inch space between the screwdriver or dipstick and the metal part of the engine. If there is no spark, there is a problem with the ignition system. This problem will require the help of a mechanic. If there is a spark for each spark-plug wire, the problem is more likely related to a lack of fuel. Check again to be sure you have enough gasoline. Turn the ignition switch to the ON position.

CAUTION: The voltage generated by modern automobile electrical systems can exceed thirty thousand volts. If you attempt to check for sparks, make sure you are protected from the electrical shock that can occur during starting and most certainly when the engine is running. Use insulated pliers, a wooden stick, or even a rolled-up floormat to hold the screwdriver or dipstick in the right position.

No Start, or Starter Cranks Slowly

Symptoms

You turn the ignition key to the start position. The starter cranks, but instead of the high-speed rotating sound you normally hear, the starter seems to be turning slowly. It might even stop and "grunt." Then it might suddenly start normally.

Explanation

Your problem lies with the starter motor, which is, for one or more of several possible reasons, not turning fast enough to start the engine. See Diagnoses and Solutions for explanations of these conditions.

Diagnoses and Solutions

One: If the engine started earlier and has been running for some time prior to shutting it off, the no-start problem might be related to a worn starter motor. Often, if you allow the engine to fully cool off it will then start normally. Ask your mechanic to test the charging system, the starter motor, and battery capacity.

Two: A weak battery and a faulty starter motor can sound the same. Try getting a boost or jump from another car battery, which can allow a faulty starter to turn fast enough to start the engine. Have the starter current draw tested before replacing the battery. You may need to have the starter motor replaced.

Three: Poor engine timing can cause a starter motor to malfunction. If you have tried the previous procedures and still the starter motor turns too slowly to start the engine, your problem is more than likely advanced timing. Have the engine timing checked.

Four: Poorly connected battery cables can cause too much resistance between the battery and the starter, reducing the flow of electrical current to the starter. Make sure the battery cable connections at the starter and the negative battery cable bolted to the engine and at the battery itself are clean and tight.

CAUTION: It is never wise to assume that, simply because a battery is too weak to start your engine, replacing it will solve the problem. Very often what might seem like a worn-out battery is actually nothing more than a loose alternator belt. Before you decide to replace the battery because of a no-start condition, read about how to check the battery and charging system on page 255, and before you attempt a jump or boost, read the precautions on page 194.

Engine Runs But Car Will Not Move (Standard Transmission)

Symptoms

You start the engine, depress the clutch pedal, and shift into gear. When you release the clutch the car does not move, no matter how hard you depress the gas pedal. You hear the engine running faster, but still the car does not move.

Explanation

A low fluid level in a manual transmission will not generally cause the transmission to malfunction. You will be able to move forward and in reverse. However, running any transmission without fluid will cause serious damage in a very short period.

Diagnoses and Solutions

One: If the car won't move forward, try shifting into reverse. If the car begins to move in the normal way, try shifting into forward again. If the car then moves forward, the problem is in the transmission linkage or in the transmission itself. A worn transmission linkage can prevent you from shifting into gear. In an emergency, try shifting into second gear instead of first.

Two: When shifting into any gear does not help, the problem is most likely a worn clutch. A clutch adjustment might help for a time, but generally the answer is replacing the clutch. In an emergency you might get home by having some friends push the car until you get rolling. Don't count on the car moving for very long. Chances are the car will not move after the next stop.

Three: In some instances the transmission cannot be

shifted into any gear despite the fact that you have depressed the clutch pedal to the floor. Try turning the engine off. If you can then shift easily, you probably need a new clutch. If the clutch pedal doesn't feel normal—that is, it moves too easily—you might have a broken clutch-pedal linkage. On cars with hydraulic clutches, a loss of fluid in the clutch master cylinder can be the problem. The first sign of a fluid loss on a standard transmission is usually a noise from the transmission. Make sure the fluid level on your standard transmission is checked every time the car is lubricated. You can recognize a car with a hydraulic clutch either by checking your owner's manual or by locating the brake master cylinder. Generally you will find a similar-looking cylinder next to the brake master cylinder. The one on the left controls the clutch. Cars with manual or nonhydraulic clutches do not have a second master cylinder.

Ignition Key Won't Come Out

Symptom

You park your car and turn off the ignition. The engine stops running, but you can't pull the ignition key out of the ignition switch.

Explanation

Ignition-switch-lock cylinders as well as door- and trunk-lock cylinders are complicated devices. They should be lubricated with small amounts of special lock lubricants such as Lock Ease or its equivalent. Lubricating lock cylinders helps to prevent the tiny pins in the lock from binding. Generally when you can't push in or remove the key it is because the pins in the lock cylinder are jammed from lack of lubricant or are broken. When you find that the feel of the lock has changed and is starting to bind, don't wait until you are stranded with a lock that won't turn. Lubricate the lock. If that doesn't help, have the lock replaced.

Diagnoses and Solutions

One: On most cars you turn the ignition switch counterclockwise until it stops to shut off the engine. If you force the key just a little harder, you might find that there is another switch position just a little farther counterclockwise than the off position. It is intended for use when you want to play the radio without having the electrical current supplied to the ignition system. Often, when an ignition-lock cylinder becomes worn, the resistance offered at the stop position is no longer as great. It becomes easy to slip past it to a point where the key cannot be removed. Should you be unable to remove the key, try turning it slightly clockwise while you also pull on the key. A new ignition-lock cylinder will repair this condition.

Two: The ignition-lock cylinder or the key might be worn to the point where the lock-cylinder pins are jamming the key in the lock. Try using a plier to grasp the key. Try to pull the key straight out of the lock. Be careful not to twist the key and break off the top. Try pushing the key in slightly, then pulling it out. Be gentle.

> **CAUTION: Automobile keys are generally made of brass, which is a relatively soft metal. They are easy to break or bend. Never use your key to pry open can lids or to cut the paper on a package. You might not notice the slight damage this can do until you try to use the key for operating its lock.**

SECTION

Steering

Power-Steering Wheel Difficult to Turn/Growling Noise

Symptom

You start the engine and attempt to turn the steering wheel. It feels as if you haven't started the engine. As you turn the wheel you hear a growling sound that gets worse as you make a full turn. It might stop when you release the steering wheel.

Explanation

You are either very low or out of power-steering fluid or have just added power-steering fluid. It is possible you have a leak somewhere in the power-steering system (also see page 248).

Diagnoses and Solutions

One: Check the power-steering pump reservoir tank for a loss of fluid. On most cars the power-steering pump and tank are located in front of the engine. On front-wheel-drive cars they are generally on the passenger side. Generally you check the power-steering fluid by removing a filler cap on the power-steering pump tank. You should be able to see the fluid or measure it with the marked dipstick attached to the tank cap. Low power-steering fluid will cause a growling noise and make the steering wheel difficult to turn. Fill the power-steering pump reservoir with approved power-steering fluid. In an emergency, use automatic-transmission fluid.

Two: If adding power-steering fluid makes the steering easier but you still hear a growl, there might be air bubbles in the fluid. It will take half an hour of driving to clear all of the air bubbles. The noise should then stop. Watch for a loss of power-steering fluid by checking the fluid level often. If there is a loss of fluid, have your mechanic find the leak.

Three: Power-steering systems don't normally lose fluid. If you find you need to add power-steering fluid between oil changes, there might be a leak at a hose, pump, or steering gear. If you are adding fluid often, have the power-steering system checked for leaks by your mechanic as soon as possible.

CAUTION: If a fluid leak occurs on the pressure side of the power-steering system it could cause a high-pressure squirt of hot fluid to be sprayed on a hot exhaust manifold or exhaust pipe. This could very easily cause a fire under the hood, which might result in the total destruction of your car and injury to you and your passengers. Do not allow a power-steering leak to go uncorrected.

Power-Steering Wheel Difficult to Turn/Squealing Noise

Symptoms

You turn the steering wheel with the engine running and you find it turns but not as easily as it should. As you turn the wheel you hear a squealing sound, as if someone had stepped on a cat's tail. When you release the steering wheel the squealing stops.

Explanation

A squeal when you turn the steering wheel on a car equipped with power steering is almost always caused by the power-steering belt slipping. The power-steering system on most cars gets its power from the engine crankshaft. The crankshaft drives a fan belt which turns the power-steering pump pulley. This pump creates the hydraulic pressure that is used to power the steering gear or the steering rack and pinion. On some cars it may also power the brakes. For the pump to work properly the fan belt driving it must be the right size, in good condition, and properly adjusted (also see page 248).

Diagnoses and Solutions

One: If the power-steering belt is in good condition, the squeal can be corrected by adjusting the belt to the proper tension. Adjusting the power-steering belt on most cars is complicated and should be done by a mechanic. If you are a serious do-it-yourself auto mechanic, it would be wise to purchase the repair-shop manual for your make and model. The shop manual provides detailed instructions on how to adjust belts, as well as most other procedures. If the belt is worn or cracked, or the inner surfaces are shiny, it should be replaced.

Two: If adjusting the power-steering belt does not stop the squeal, it might be that the belt is too long and can't be adjusted. Have your mechanic install a new belt of the proper length.

Three: A loose or broken power-steering mounting bracket or one on which bolts are missing can prevent the belt from being fully tightened. Consult your mechanic for this repair.

CAUTION: Always disconnect one of the battery cables whenever you attempt to adjust the power-steering or any other belt. By disconnecting the battery you eliminate the possibility of the engine starting and causing injury to your hands. Should you happen to touch a wire, having the battery disconnected will prevent any serious damage caused by a short circuit.

Steering Wheel Not Centered

Symptoms

Your car steers normally, but when you drive straight ahead on a long straight section of the road, you find that the steering wheel is not centered. The spokes of the wheel that should be level when you are driving straight ahead are not. You might have to hold the steering wheel as if you were making a slight turn to the left or right for the car to run straight ahead.

Explanation

Steering-wheel position is one important element of wheel alignment. When you turn the steering wheel you are actually turning a shaft in either a steering gearbox or a rack-and-pinion steering assembly. The steering gearbox or rack-and-pinion steering assembly transmits that movement you apply to the steering wheel to each of the front wheels through steel rods called tie rods. The tie rods link the wheels to the movement of the steering wheel. The system of tie rods and the fittings on the ends of the tie rods make up the steering linkage. When one or more of these tie rods are damaged or well worn, the steering wheel is no longer centered. One of the adjustments done during a wheel alignment is to center the steering wheel (also see pages 233, 248).

Diagnoses and Solutions

One: The most likely reason your steering wheel is not centered when you drive straight ahead is that the wheels are out of alignment. All it takes is a pothole or a bang against the curb to knock the wheels out of alignment. Centering the steering wheel is important because the steering system is designed for the steering wheel to be centered when the car is going straight ahead. This condition may also indicate additional wheel-alignment problems, and should be inspected by a mechanic.

Two: As you drive, move the steering wheel left, then right, to see if the car responds immediately to the steering. If you find that the car seems to still go straight as you turn, there might be dangerous wear in the steering linkage or steering gearbox. To check for this, set the parking brake and make sure you have shifted the transmission into park. Leave the engine running. Open the left front window. Exit from the car and position yourself so that you are standing next to the left front door, facing the front of the car. Reach in with your right hand and move the steering wheel. As you move the wheel from the straight-ahead position to the left and then to the right, watch the left front tire. It should move left or right at nearly the instant you move the steering wheel. If you find there is considerable movement of the steering wheel before the tire starts turning, have your mechanic check for a worn steering linkage or problems in the steering gearbox.

Three: If the steering wheel is suddenly no longer centered after an accident, there might be damage to the steering linkage. This might also occur after you have driven up onto a curb or road divider, into a pothole, or after your car has gone through a car wash. Have your mechanic check the steering linkage for damage.

CAUTION: Centering the steering wheel should be done from under the car. Be wary if a mechanic attempts to center your steering wheel by removing the steering wheel from inside the car and reinstalling it with the wheels in the straight-ahead position. There might be a serious problem that has not been corrected during the wheel alignment.

Car Drifts to One Side While Steering Wheel Is Centered

Symptoms

You're driving on a straight and level road and find that you seem to be drifting either to the left or right. Unlike a brake pull that occurs only when you step on the brake, this condition feels as if you are steering the car to one side when actually you are steering straight ahead. You need to steer in the opposite direction just to keep the car going straight.

Explanation

For many years the major area of concern during a wheel alignment was the front wheels. This was mainly because the rear wheels on most cars rarely went out of alignment, due to the nature of construction. Most rear-wheel-drive cars were heavy and solid, and unless they were in a major accident the rear alignment did not need to be adjusted; nor could it be easily adjusted. The advent of front-wheel-drive cars with independent front and rear suspensions has created a need for aligning all four wheels. A growing number of front-wheel-drive cars now have the adjustment capability and require all four wheels to be checked during an alignment. Where there is the capability for adjusting all four wheels, you should make sure you are actually getting a four-wheel alignment. This requires special equipment and know-how on the part of the mechanic doing the alignment. You can also expect to pay a higher price for a true four-wheel alignment than for a two-wheel (also see pages 233, 248).

Diagnoses and Solutions

One: Most often a steering pull to one side is caused by a wheel-alignment problem. There are strict factory specifications for the position of the wheels on the front and rear of every car. When one of the wheels is tilted inward or outward too much or the wheels are not exactly parallel, the car steers to one side. This can also occur if the rear wheels are not aligned to properly follow the front wheels. Either way, your car will need to have an alignment check. Late model cars will need a four-wheel alignment.

Two: Check the air in all of the tires. Low air pressure in one of the front tires will cause the steering to veer to one side. Make sure too that all of the tires are of the same size and style. If, for example, you were to install a tire marked P205/75R15 on one front tire while the other tire was marked P205/70R15MS, chances are the car would steer toward the latter's side. It really doesn't matter what type of tire or to which side the car pulls. The important thing is to understand that an underinflated or a different type of tire can cause a steering pull.

Three: In some instances, a car steers either to the right or left because one of the front brakes is dragging. This can be caused by one of the front disc-brake calipers jamming, preventing the brake from fully releasing. This can easily be checked by jacking up the wheels and rotating each tire by hand. The wheels should turn freely. Make sure the transmission is in neutral and the parking brake is released for this test.

CAUTION: You can generally recognize that a mechanic is actually doing a four-wheel alignment when the equipment includes a fixture that attaches to each of the four wheels. Most four-wheel-alignment equipment is clearly marked that it is designed to measure the alignment on all four wheels. It is probably also marked "computerized."

Steering Wheel Vibrates at Low Speed

Symptoms

As you drive at ten or fifteen miles per hour, you feel the steering wheel moving under your hands. It feels almost as if someone were actually pulling the steering wheel in the opposite direction of where you wanted it to go. While the pull seems to come at regular intervals as the car moves, it cannot actually be called a vibration.

Explanation

Although it might appear that tires are a mass of rubber molded as one piece, in actual fact tires are really made up of layers of rubber. The layers are put into a mold to form the shape and tire tread. When a tire bulges it is because something has caused the tire layers to separate. Air pressure seeping into the separation forms a balloon. Sometimes this occurs when a nail punctures the tire, then pushes through to form a new hole in the inner tire wall. Hitting a pothole can also break the inner tire wall and allow air to enter.

Sometimes the tire layers separate because of a defect in manufacture. Regardless of how it happens, a defect in the way the tire layers are fused to each other will result in a bulge, a waddle, and eventually a tire failure (also see pages 230, 233, 248).

Diagnoses and Solutions

One: Get something to kneel on and that will keep your knees clean. Get down and take a careful look at each of your tires. Check the treads and both the inside and outside tire walls. Move the car about five feet forward and do it again. Make sure you look over the entire surface of all of the tires. What you are looking for is a bulge in the wall or tire tread. Before a blowout, the interior wall of a tire may break, allowing air pressure to get between the inner and outer tire wall. This air pressure forms a bulge, which will make the steering wheel jump or move each time the bulge hits the pavement. In extreme cases a section of the tire tread might have already broken off, leaving a section of tire without any tread. The presence of a bulge or missing section of tire tread means a blowout or flat is imminent. Install your spare tire or get to a tire-repair shop as soon as possible.

Two: If you do not find a bulge or missing section of tread, have your mechanic put the car on a lift. Carefully check the tire treads to make sure they are uniform. As a tire is rotated you might find that the tread does not appear to be even in one or more areas. The tire-tread pattern may seem to be pulled slightly to one side. This is called a tire waddle. You may feel it in the steering wheel; if it is a rear tire, you will feel the seat of the car sort of move from side to side under you as you drive at low speeds. You might not feel it at higher speeds. When a tire has a waddle, it is because the tire tread has moved to one side of the body of the tire. The remedy is to replace the tire.

Three: What might feel like a steering wheel vibration can be caused by loose wheel bearings. This is generally not a problem on front-wheel-drive cars, but it can occur on rear-wheel-drive cars. If the tires are good yet you feel the steering wheel vibrate at low speeds, ask your mechanic to check the front wheel bearings.

Steering Wheel Vibrates at Highway Speeds

Symptoms

Your tires are in good condition and free of bulges and damaged treads. Yet when you drive at certain speeds over twenty-five miles per hour, you feel the steering wheel suddenly begin to vibrate. Sometimes the vibration is only very slight. Other times the vibration creates a thundering sound that only stops when you slow the car down.

Explanation

At high speeds the balance of each wheel and tire becomes very important. If wheels are out of balance, they begin to vibrate. This vibration is transmitted to the steering linkage and the suspension that holds the wheels to the car. The service life of the front and rear suspension is greatly reduced when a wheel-balance vibration is left unrepaired. A wheel-balance vibration also causes premature tire wear, tire-tread damage, and premature tire failure (also see pages 230, 233, 248).

Diagnoses and Solutions

One: When you feel the steering wheel vibrate in your hands as you drive at highway speeds, it often means that one wheel and tire combination is out of balance. This means there is a spot on one part of the tire that is heavier than a similar spot on the other side of the tire. As the speed increases, the heavier spot tends to cause a vibration. This is known as a wheel-balance vibration. Having a mechanic balance the wheel usually corrects the problem. It is generally a good idea to have every new tire balanced. When a vibration occurs, have all four wheels balanced.

Two: A vibration similar to a wheel-balance problem can occur when a tire is not truly round or when there is a slight, almost undetectable bulge in the tire tread. Generally this condition also causes a thump at low speeds. You might also feel the car moving up and down as the wheel turns. The cure is to replace the offending tire. A tire that is not truly round can easily be detected by a mechanic on a wheel-balancing machine, where it is possible to see the exact shape as the tire is slowly turned.

Three: A wheel and tire might also vibrate as a result of a collision or impact with a pothole that causes the wheel to be bent out of its original shape. Generally wheel balancing will not correct the vibration caused by a bent wheel. A bent wheel is easily detected on a wheel-balancing machine, and will generally need to be replaced if found to be bent.

Car Drifts to One Side When Braking

Symptoms

You drive on a straight and level road and the car steers normally until you step on the brake pedal. At that moment the car steers either to the right or left. It feels as if you have turned the steering wheel, when in fact you have kept steering straight ahead. In order for you to come to a straight stop, you have to steer the car in the opposite direction when you apply the brakes.

Explanation

When you step on the brake pedal you cause the hydraulic pressure to increase at the brakes at each of the four wheels. The front brakes generally do most of the braking, so a defect in the front is usually more noticeable. As the hydraulic pressure increases, the disc-brake calipers squeeze the brake pads against the brake drums. To accomplish a smooth, even stop, both calipers must squeeze with the same amount of pressure. A rusted or worn-out brake caliper can drag and not squeeze the brake pads. Worn brake pads can cause the same symptom. The quality of brake pads makes a difference in the amount of friction they provide. Brake calipers should be checked for leaks and for binding any time the brakes are checked or whenever you detect a brake problem (see page 252).

Diagnoses and Solutions

One: The moment you detect a pull to one side each time you apply the brakes, reduce your speed to make controlling the car easier. If you are on a highway, pull off as soon as possible to a lesser road with lower speeds. Mechanics call this problem a brake pull. Keep a close eye on the instrument panel brake-warning light. Very often a brake pull is accompanied by a loss of brake fluid, which will eventually cause the brake-warning light to go on. Most often the pull occurs when one of the front brakes is not functioning properly. To find the cause of the pull or brake fluid loss you will need the services of a competent brake mechanic.

Two: Trouble in a rear-wheel brake might also cause a brake pull to one side. Generally a brake pull caused by a rear-wheel brake problem is less noticeable than a problem caused by a front-wheel brake. Don't allow this condition to persist. See a competent brake mechanic as soon as possible. In the meantime, drive slowly and be careful.

CAUTION: Although it is important to slow down to gain better control of a car with a brake defect such as a brake pull, it is also important to remember that driving too slowly on a fast highway can actually be more dangerous. Use good judgment when you detect a brake pull. Move to the slow lane, switch on your emergency flashers, and slow down to a safe speed. You will probably be able to safely drive to the nearest repair facility, provided you allow extra room for stopping and keep your speed down.

Car Drifts to One Side While Accelerating or Decelerating

Symptoms

Unlike a wheel-alignment problem, where the car drifts either right or left when you loosely grasp the steering wheel, or a brake problem in which the car drifts to one side or the other when you step on the brake, this problem causes the car to drift to one side as you accelerate and then to the opposite side when you decelerate.

Explanation

Be careful about snap judgments when it comes to trying to determine why a particular car has a tendency to drift to one side when accelerating or decelerating. Unless the dog bones or motor mounts are obviously worn, don't assume that replacing them will be a guaranteed cure. I have driven some powerful sports cars for which torque steer is just a function of the tremendous power applied to the wheels and is not easily eliminated. The rule to follow about attempting to cure torque steer is to determine if the problem was with the car from day one or if it has recently developed. If the latter is the case, you have a good chance of correcting the problem. If it came with the car brand new, you might never eliminate it because of a design weakness on some cars. Before you simply accept it, contact the customer service department for the manufacturer of your car. There may be a technical service bulletin dealing with the problem on your particular make and model car.

Diagnoses and Solutions

One: When a car drifts either right or left as you step on the gas, the problem is generally known as torque steer. When you step on the gas and apply power or torque to the rear wheels, you feel a reaction in the steering. Generally the car steers in the opposite direction as you reduce speed. The first place to have a mechanic look for the cause of this problem is in the engine stabilizers, generally known as dog bones mount. A dog bone mount is really a bracket used to keep the engine from twisting either too far forward or too far to the rear when power is applied on a front-wheel-drive car. Torque steer often results when a dog-bone engine stabilizer develops wear at the two rubber bushings on either end. This problem might also occur if the rubber motor mounts that actually hold the engine and transaxle assembly in place in the body break, become worn, or soften.

Two: Torque steer can also develop as the result of a collision in which the engine-transaxle alignment is changed. If you have had a collision, have a mechanic check this if you are experiencing torque steer.

Three: A problem with the front drive axles could also contribute to the tendency for a front-wheel-drive car to drift to one side or the other. When you have eliminated the other possible causes, have a mechanic check for this problem.

Car Sways from Side to Side or Waddles

Symptoms

As you drive down the driveway or slowly up the street, you feel the seat under you swaying from side to side. When you increase speed, the sway becomes less noticeable. You might also feel the steering wheel moving under your hands. This condition is generally known as a waddle, because the car seems to be moving like a duck walks.

Explanation

You are feeling some type of defect in a tire.

Diagnoses and Solutions

One: Check all of the tires for obvious bumps or bulges (see page 230). If you see a section of the tire ballooning out, this could be causing the problem. A tire with this type of damage must be replaced. Install the spare before you drive to a tire dealer.

Two: The cause of a waddle can be less obvious than a visible bulge or ballooning of a tire. Often the steel or fabric cords within the tire break or shift. This causes the shape of the tire to change. Instead of a straight-line pattern, the shifted cords cause the tire tread to be uneven. To observe this condition and actually find the tire causing the waddle, it is best to either jack up each wheel separately or get the car up on a lift where the wheels hang freely. Rotate each wheel while you look at the tread portion of the tire. On a good tire, the tread will appear even and you will not see any obvious change in the straight-line pattern as you rotate the tire. Where there is a broken tire, you will see the pattern of the tire tread suddenly jump to one side as you rotate the tire. Here again, there is no repair other than replacing the tire. See the section Get to Know Your Tires (see page 230).

CAUTION: When a tire is cut, broken, worn, or ballooning, the sharp ends of steel wire might be protruding from the tire tread. Be careful not to run your hand across the tread area. The broken steel wire could cause a nasty cut.

Brakes

Brakes Make Grinding
Sound When Stopping

Symptoms

Your car runs normally, but when you depress the brake pedal you hear and feel a grinding noise. When you release the brake pedal, the grinding noise stops. In some instances depressing the brake pedal might cause the car to veer to one side or the other.

Explanation

A grinding noise while braking is not something to be taken lightly. It is not the type of problem you should allow to continue for any longer than it takes to get to a mechanic. When the friction material of the brake pads or brake shoes is worn so thin that the brakes grind, the braking efficiency is greatly reduced. If the car veers to one side while braking, it could cause you to lose control of the car. The brakes might also lock up and cause a skid. More important, you simply cannot stop as well when the friction material is worn away. A further word about replacing brakes: There are some very good brands of brake pads and brake lining available. There are also some very poor-quality brakes available. Before you agree to a brake job, ask your mechanic what brand of brakes he will be installing. Ask about the warranty. Better-quality brakes will often have a lifetime warranty. A call to one or two local auto-supply stores will give you an idea of the quality of the brand your mechanic plans to use. Relined brakes mean that you will be getting old brake shoes with new friction material. Better-quality brakes have new brake shoes with new brake linings or pads. Save any warranty papers carefully (see page 252).

Diagnoses and Solutions

One: Open your car windows and drive slowly near a wall or a row of parked cars. The sound will bounce off the wall or parked cars and give you some idea of whether it is from the front or rear wheels. Generally the front brakes wear first, so, chances are the noise will be from the front. However, it is important to have all four wheels removed and all of the brakes checked whenever you hear a noise related to braking. When a grinding noise occurs during braking, it generally means that the brake-pad or brake-shoe friction material has worn so thin that the metal rivets or steel backing plates are directly exposed to the brake rotors or drums. In other words, there is metal-to-metal contact between the brake pads and the rotors or between the brake shoes and the brake drums. This sort of contact quickly damages the surface of the rotors or drums. Slight damage can usually be corrected by machining a rotor or drum surface on a brake lathe. Mechanics often refer to this as cutting the rotors or drums, as it involves cutting metal away to create a new smooth surface. There is a legal limit to how much metal can be removed. If the damage is beyond the legal limit, the rotors or drums will have to be replaced.

Two: Check the red brake warning light on your instrument panel. This light warns of trouble in the brake hydraulic system. It will go on when there is a brake-fluid loss. It might also go on when the rear brakes are badly worn. A grinding noise accompanied by the red brake warning light might be caused by worn or misadjusted rear brake shoes. Have your mechanic check the brakes for wear and adjust or replace brakes as needed.

Brakes Squeal

Symptoms

When you depress the brake pedal you hear a squealing sound, most often from the front of the car. It usually occurs just before the car comes to a stop. A brake squeal should not be confused with a brake grind discussed earlier. A grind is a harsh, low-pitched rubbing sound. A squeal is a much higher-pitched sound that you will not feel through the steering wheel or brake pedal. It most often occurs when you brake lightly.

Explanation

Brake squeal is more common on imported cars. However, it can occur on any car with either disc brakes or drum brakes, or a combination of disc brakes in the front and drum brakes in the rear. The squealing noise is caused by the brake pad moving across the brake rotor. It's much the same as rubbing your finger over the top of a fine wineglass. Correcting the vibration usually stops the squeal. Various devices are used. Soft paste or a stick-on insulator most often dampens the vibration and stops the noise. In some cases the brake pads might be poorly fitted to the brake caliper. This condition might require a simple adjustment or replacement of the brake pads or hardware (see page 252).

Diagnoses and Solutions

One: Brake lightly as you come to a slow stop. Next, brake more aggressively. If you find the squeal to be more obvious when you brake lightly, the problem is more annoying than serious. Assuming the brake pads are in good condition, it can generally be corrected by having a mechanic install a special paste to the back of the brake pads. If the noise is present even during hard braking, more involved repairs might be needed. You might have to switch to a different type of brake pad or brake lining. A new brake-pad antirattle kit may also be available to correct this problem. Check with the car dealer or the parts department of an auto-supply store.

Two: Take careful note of when the squeal occurs. If the squeal occurs as you drive but stops when you step on the brake pedal, you are probably hearing what is called the low brake warning. On many cars there is a device that emits a squealing sound when the front brake pads are worn. The squeal stops when you step on the brakes. When you hear a low brake-warning squeal, it means your brakes should be checked by a mechanic as soon as possible.

Brake Pedal Pulses When Stopping

Symptoms

The car acts as if you were pressing, then releasing, the brake as you come to a stop. The brake pedal might feel as if it were pushing back under your foot.

Explanation

There are several theories as to why a disc-brake rotor warps. They include overtightening of the lug nuts, sudden cooling of the brake rotors, abuse of the brakes, and a buildup of resin from inferior brake pads. Whatever the reason, the solution is generally cutting the rotor. However, you should be aware that not all brake rotors can safely be cut. This is particularly true of imported cars with vented disc-brake rotors. There are specified limits as to the amount of metal that can be safely removed from a brake rotor or drum.

Diagnoses and Solutions

One: Find a deserted street to check this condition. Drive straight ahead and slowly depress the brake pedal. Try it first at ten miles per hour, then again a little faster. When the brakes are normal, you should feel an even pressure on the brake pedal. In a condition where the brake pedal pulses, you will feel the brake pedal moving under your foot. The faster you drive, the more pronounced will be the pulsation when you depress the brake pedal. In extreme cases you might feel the vibration through the steering wheel. The pulsation you feel is caused by a condition mechanics generally refer to as warped disc-brake rotors. Most often this condition can be corrected by having a mechanic cut or replace the brake rotors.

Two: The brake pedal can also pulse on cars equipped with brake drums. Older cars might have brake drums in the front, although most often you will find disc brakes in the front and drum brakes in the rear. Modern luxury cars and high-performance cars are likely to have disc brakes on all four wheels. A brake pedal can also pulse if a brake drum has gone out of shape. If the drum is oval, instead of perfectly round, the brakes will pulse. Having the drum cut or replaced should solve the problem.

CAUTION: Whenever metal is cut from a brake rotor or drum, the part is weakened to some extent. Cutting within the specified limit is safe. However, cutting more than that amount will weaken the rotor or drum. It will also cause the brakes to operate at higher temperatures. Be sure to ask your mechanic about the safety of cutting a brake drum or rotor. In many cases a new rotor costs only about a third more than cutting an old rotor. Some brake rotors may have a special heat treatment and cannot be cut at all. Check with the car maker's customer service department to determine if the brake rotors on your car cannot be machined (see page 252).

Brake Pedal Fades When Braking

Symptoms

When you hold your foot on the brake, the pedal drops away under your foot and might even fade completely to the floor.

Explanation

Assuming there is no loss of brake fluid, the most common reason for a brake pedal to fade is an internal leak in the brake master cylinder. Before replacing the master cylinder, your mechanic should carefully check the brakes on all four wheels for fluid leaks. The mechanic should also check the brake hoses and metal brake lines for leaks, for air in the system, and for rear brakes in need of adjustment (see page 252).

Diagnoses and Solutions

One: Normally your brake pedal should be firm to the touch. When you reach the bottom of the brake pedal's travel, as you would when you are stopping for a traffic light, the pedal should stay firm under your foot. If you find that the brake pedal seems to fade or melt away under your foot, drive the car slowly for a few yards, then brake. When the car comes to a full stop, keep your foot depressed on the brake pedal. Count to sixty. If you feel the pedal sort of melting away under your foot, keep the same pressure on the pedal. Check to see if the pedal fades to the floor. If the car starts to roll forward, pump the brake pedal once or twice to stop the car. In an emergency you can drive home safely, provided you are ready to quickly release then reapply the brake pedal. This is called pumping the brakes. Have a competent brake mechanic bleed any air out of the hydraulic system and repair or replace the master cylinder.

Two: Check the level of brake fluid in the master cylinder. On most cars the master cylinder is located on the bulkhead near the left side. There are two brake-fluid reservoirs in most modern master cylinders. The cover must be removed to check the fluid level (it is easy to check). Both should be full to about half an inch from the top of the master cylinder. One low chamber is your clue to a brake-fluid loss. When the brake fluid gets low enough in the master cylinder, air is pumped into the brake hydraulic system. Air in the system can cause the brake pedal to fade and feel spongy or soft. The brake warning light will generally glow when there is a major loss of brake fluid. Have a brake mechanic find the leak.

Brake Pedal Too Low

Symptoms

The height of the brake pedal above the floor is suddenly less than it used to be. There is little, if any, pedal reserve —the distance from the pedal to the floor.

Explanation

In order for a brake pedal to be at its proper height, the brakes must be properly adjusted. On front disc brakes this is generally not a problem, because the normal action of the disc-brake pistons causes them to automatically adjust. That is, as long as the disc-brake caliper pistons are not corroded and binding. However, the rear disc brakes on some cars are sometimes the cause of a low brake pedal. If your car has rear disc brakes and a lower than normal brake pedal, it might be wise to remind your mechanic that the parking-brake mechanism in some rear disc brakes can malfunction and cause a low brake pedal. On cars with drum brakes, the problem is generally caused by the need for a brake adjustment or by worn brakes (see page 252).

Diagnoses and Solutions

One: Brake-pedal height varies from one model of car to another. What might be a too-low brake pedal for one model might be normal for another. The thing to watch for is a change in pedal height. If suddenly you realize that the brake pedal is lower than it normally had been, it is cause for concern. Most often a brake pedal will be lower when the rear wheel brakes are in need of adjustment. On modern cars the brakes adjust automatically, usually when you step on the brake in reverse. First try backing up the car and braking. Do this two or three times in a deserted place, where you won't risk hitting another car or a pedestrian. The brake pedal will probably get higher. If it doesn't, the rear brake self-adjuster mechanism might not be working. There might also be wear on the rear brakes. If the brake-pedal height is still too low, have your mechanic remove all four wheels and check the brakes.

Two: Adjusting rear drum brakes will most often correct the problem. A low brake pedal can also occur where there is air trapped in the brake hydraulic system. To rid the system of air, a mechanic must bleed the brake system using a special bleeder valve located at each wheel.

Parking Brake Won't Release

Symptoms

When you release the parking brake, the parking-brake warning light stays on or the parking-brake pedal stays down.

Explanation

When you employ the parking brake, what you are really doing is pulling on a series of cables that on most cars locks the brakes on the rear wheels. After years of exposure to water, salt, and all sorts of road dirt, the cables can become damaged. Often a cable seizes and will not move. If the cable seizes in the off position, the parking brake will not apply. If it seizes in the on position, you might have released the parking-brake lever, yet still be riding with the rear brakes partially applied. You can tell when this happens because it will be more difficult for the car to roll; that is, you will have to exert more pressure on the gas pedal to move the car. When you coast to a stop, the car will feel as if you have applied the brakes without your actually touching the brake pedal. When the parking-brake cable breaks, operating the parking brake will have no effect.

Diagnoses and Solutions

One: On cars that have a parking-brake release handle located to the left of the steering wheel, when the foot-operated parking brake won't release, the problem is often a broken or disconnected release cable. You can release this type of manual parking brake by looking under the dash at the parking-brake mechanism. There is usually a small lever to which the release cable is attached. Use a screwdriver or pliers to try to move the lever. When you release it, the parking pedal will snap up, releasing the parking brake. You will need a new parking-brake release cable or a new park brake assembly.

Two: On cars where the parking brake releases automatically when you move the shift lever to the drive position, there is nearly always a small lever you can pull to release the parking brake. To find it you will have to reach under the dash to the left. The release lever is attached to the upper part of the parking-brake mechanism. The problem might be a disconnected vacuum hose, a leaking neutral safety switch, or a defective parking-brake release mechanism.

Three: On cars where the parking brake is operated by a lever located to the left of the driver's seat or between the two front seats, you might have to also pull the parking-brake lever slightly while depressing the release button located on the handle. Check your owner's manual for the correct procedure to release the parking brake—the technique varies from one make to another. Then if it won't release, see your mechanic.

CAUTION: Don't think of your parking brake as an emergency brake. The term *emergency brake* goes back to the days when the extra brake really was a powerful brake that could be used when the regular brakes didn't work. On modern cars, the regular brakes have built-in safety features and the parking brake is intended principally for parking on level ground. Don't depend on it on a hill. Always turn your wheels all the way to the left or right, whichever will guide the car away from traffic should the brake fail. Generally, the curb will keep your car from rolling more than a few inches.

Brake Pedal Difficult to Depress (Power Brakes)

Symptoms

You step on the brake pedal, and instead of it moving down with light pressure from your foot, it feels like it won't move. It feels as if you haven't yet started the engine.

Explanation

The vast majority of power-brake systems use engine-manifold vacuum to power the brakes. If you suspect that your vacuum-operated power brake isn't working, here is a simple test: Turn off the ignition key and pump the brake pedal several times. Now depress the brake pedal and hold it down. Start the engine. As you start the engine, if the power brake is working, you will feel the brake pedal suddenly move downward. If the power brake is not working, it will not move as the engine is started. Remember that the power brake is a power assist. If it fails, you will still have brakes. They will be much more difficult to depress, but if you press hard enough you will be able to stop the car (also see page 252).

Diagnoses and Solutions

One: If your brake pedal suddenly becomes difficult to depress while you are driving, your first course of action would be to press the brake pedal harder than normal to slow the car. Most often a hard brake pedal is the result of a power-brake failure. On most cars the power brakes are run on engine vacuum. For the brakes to work normally, there must be engine vacuum at the power-brake assembly. If the rubber hose between the engine intake manifold and the brake assembly were to come off, there would be no vacuum. It is easy to spot the power-brake vacuum hose. It generally attaches to the power-brake assembly, which is bolted to the back of the engine-compartment wall (fire wall) just in front of the driver. The brake master cylinder is bolted onto the power brake. When the vacuum hose to the power brake becomes disconnected, you will hear a shriek or sucking sound as air rushes into the open end of the hose. The engine idle will also be affected and the engine might run faster than normal at idle.

Two: If you do not hear the sound of air rushing into an open or disconnected vacuum hose, the problem might be a clogged hose. You can test for this by disconnecting the hose at the power brake assembly (see solution One). You should hear and feel the pull of vacuum at the end of the hose. If you don't feel vacuum, the other end of the hose, where it attaches to the engine, might be disconnected or clogged. If you have no vacuum at the hose and can find nothing causing it, you will need the help of a mechanic to determine if the problem is the power brake or check valve. If the check valve is good, chances are you will need a new power-brake assembly.

Three: Some cars have a power brake that does not run on vacuum from the engine. The hydroboost system, for instance, is powered by hydraulic fluid pressure from the power-steering pump. On this system, a loss of power-steering fluid can cause hard steering and a loss of power braking. A broken power-steering-pump belt will cause a loss of power steering and power braking. Have a brake mechanic check for leaks, pressure loss, or mechanical failure. Another type of power brake uses an electric motor to create hydraulic pressure for the brakes. On this type, a blown fuse or electrical problem could cause a loss of power braking. Beyond that, see a competent brake mechanic for a diagnosis.

CAUTION: Do not ignore an intermittent hard brake problem. If you have had an experience where the brake pedal suddenly became hard to depress, then worked normally, do not assume the problem has been corrected. Have your mechanic carefully check the brake system and don't be satisfied until the problem has been corrected.

Brakes Grab or Lock

Symptoms

You step on the brake pedal to bring the car to a normal stop, then suddenly the brakes seem to have a mind of their own. The brakes apply as if you have stomped on the brake pedal.

Explanation

For the brakes to work normally, there must be good, clean contact between the brake pads and the disc-brake rotor or, on drum-brake systems, between the brake lining and the brake drum. Where there is any contamination such as rust, dirt, water, grease, or brake fluid present between the surfaces of the brake pads and the surface of the brake rotor, there will be a brake problem (see page 252).

Diagnoses and Solutions

One: When front brake pads are worn thin or to a point where the metal of the brake-pad backing plate and the metal of the brake rotor meet face to face, the brake can grab. You might also feel the car drift to the left or right as you brake. It might drift left then right, or the opposite. Along with the grab and brake pull, you might hear a grinding noise as the metal-to-metal contact occurs. The solution is to have the brake pads replaced and possibly the brake rotors replaced or machined.

Two: If this condition occurs immediately after having the brakes repaired, it might be caused by an incorrect adjustment of the master cylinder. Allow the brakes to cool and bring the car back to the repair shop as soon as possible.

Three: On any car with rear-wheel drum brakes and rear-wheel drive, it is possible for grease from the differential (rear axle) to leak past the grease seals and onto the brake lining. When this happens, the braking efficiency of the grease-covered wheel is reduced and the brake will often grab or lock. You might be able to confirm this by looking under the car at the inside wall of the rear tires. When there is a grease leak on the rear brakes, you will usually see evidence of grease on the inside tire wall and on the lower edge of the brake backing plate. Smaller quantities of grease may leak from a front-wheel-drive car when the wheel grease retainers fail. Have your mechanic check the leaks and replace the defective grease retainers.

Four: A leaking disc-brake caliper or drum-brake wheel cylinder might leak and allow brake fluid to coat the brake pads or lining. This, too, can cause the brakes to grab or lock. The loss of brake fluid will also cause the instrument-panel brake-warning light to come on.

CAUTION: Any car that has been unused for several months or longer can develop rusty brake rotors or drums. This can cause the brakes to be less efficient during the first hundred miles of driving. If the brakes are inefficient, it would be wise to have your mechanic remove all four wheels and carefully check the complete brake system, and flush out all of the old brake fluid and replace it.

Brake Pedal Is Soft or Spongy

Symptoms

You step on the brake pedal and the car stops, but the brake pedal doesn't feel as firm as it normally does. It feels almost as if there is a soft sponge between your foot and the brake pedal. On some stops you might have to pump the pedal to get the car to stop quickly enough.

Explanation

When air becomes trapped anywhere in the brake hydraulic system, it acts like a cushion. As you depress the pedal, the air compresses. The space occupied by the air bubble is reduced and the pressure in the system is reduced. This acts to reduce the pressure on the brake calipers and wheel cylinders. The result is that instead of the pedal being firm, as it should be, it is soft because the bubbles or air cushion the pressure. The only way to remove air from the brake system is through bleeding the hydraulic system. When a mechanic bleeds your brake system he is purging air from the system. When you have the brake system bled, instruct your mechanic to replace all of the brake fluid. Brake fluid can absorb moisture over time, which can create rust in the fluid, which can boil during a period of hard braking. Boiling brake fluid will cause brake failure (see page 252).

Diagnoses and Solutions

One: If you discover the brake pedal is soft while you are driving on the highway, increase the distance you maintain between your car and the car in front. A soft brake pedal might be caused by a loss of brake fluid. Keep an eye on the instrument-panel brake-warning light, which will turn on to indicate a loss of brake fluid. When the brake pedal is soft or spongy underfoot, you will generally be able to stop the car. However, if you feel the pedal traveling too far down before a stop, try pumping the brake pedal. As soon as it is possible to do so safely, move to the slow lane and switch on your four-way emergency warning lights. Slow down to a reasonably safe speed that will allow you more control yet prevent you from blocking traffic. Check the brake fluid; add fluid if needed. Have a mechanic bleed the brake hydraulic system and find the reason why the brake fluid was lost.

Two: If, after the brake system has been checked for visible brake-fluid leaks, the brake pedal is still soft or spongy, the brake hydraulic system will need to be bled. Bleeding the brake system is simply a way of removing bubbles of air that have found their way into the brake hydraulic system. You will need a mechanic for this job. It requires special tools and might require the use of a pressure-bleeder device that pumps hydraulic pressure into the brake system.

Three: If the brake pedal feels a little spongy immediately after new brake pads or linings have been installed, don't be alarmed, provided you can stop the car safely at all speeds. There is a short break-in period, during which the brakes might feel slightly spongy or soft. This break-in period should not last more than a day or two in normal city driving. If the brakes do not feel normal return to your mechanic as soon as possible.

CAUTION: Be very careful about adding brake fluid to your brake master cylinder. Read the label twice to be sure that it is actually brake fluid and not power-steering fluid that you are adding to the master cylinder. Pouring in the wrong type of fluid is a common and costly error made by many car owners. Use only DOT-approved brake fluid. (See page 254 for precautions about brake fluid.) If you can remove a radiator cap, you should be able to learn to check your master cylinder. On most cars it is located on the bulkhead to the left side of the car. It may have a screw-off cap or a cover that must be released. Check your owner's manual, or ask your mechanic to show you how to check the brake fluid the next time you have your car lubricated. It is smart to check your brake fluid when you do your monthly fluid-levels check or before a long trip.

Brakes Do Not Release/Brakes Drag

Symptoms

When driving, you seem to have to press harder than normal on the gas pedal to make the car move. As you drive along and release the gas pedal, the car rolls to a stop sooner than normal. It feels as if you have your foot lightly pressed on the brake, yet you do not have your foot anywhere near the pedal.

Explanation

A mechanical problem is causing partial pressure to be applied by the brakes. See Diagnoses and Solutions for explanations of possible causes.

Diagnoses and Solutions

One: Check the parking brake. You might never use the parking brake because you depend on the park position of the automatic transmission to keep the car from rolling. It might be that someone drove your car and used the parking brake. Try re-releasing the parking brake and see if that helps.

Two: Over time, the cable that operates the parking brake can become rusted. When this occurs, the parking brake can jam in the on position. This might not be noticeable because the parking-brake lever or pedal seems to work normally. What is happening is that the rear brakes are not releasing because the cable has seized. This will result in brake drag and eventually premature wear on the rear brakes. You might also detect a strong odor, like the smell of burning electrical wiring. Have your mechanic check for worn brakes and binding park cables.

Three: The disc-brake calipers must squeeze the brake pads to stop the car. When you release the brake pedal, the caliper pistons must recede back into the calipers to take the pressure off the brake pads. When they do not recede, the brakes remain applied. This will cause the wheels to drag as if you were still pressing on the brake pedal. If both front brake calipers drag, the problem might be in the master cylinder. If only one brake caliper drags, the car drifts to one side. See your mechanic about rebuilding or replacing the dragging brake calipers.

Four: Brakes that drag soon after installation might be adjusted improperly. If a new master cylinder has been installed, the problem might be in the adjustment of the master-cylinder push rod. This is the rod that connects the brake pedal to the master cylinder. If it is too long, the brakes might not fully release. This condition can also cause the brake fluid to overheat and the brakes to fade. You should bring the car back to the mechanic who replaced or adjusted the master cylinder or brakes. A simple adjustment may correct the problem.

CAUTION: Whenever brake repairs are done, be alert to any unusual conditions afterward. If you feel the pedal is soft, spongy, hard to depress, or if the car doesn't stop as well as you believe it should, return it to your mechanic as soon as possible. Ask him to road test the car with you so you can demonstrate your concerns.

IV

Warning Lights

Check-Engine Warning Light

Symptoms

With the engine running, the yellow check-engine warning light on the instrument panel turns on and stays on. You probably do not feel any symptoms and wonder why the light is on. If you're like many drivers, you assume there is a problem with the wiring and dismiss this warning. You do not have to pull to the side of the road or even go directly to a repair shop when the yellow check-engine light goes on, but you should not ignore it.

Explanation

The onboard computer system on any modern car is based on a central computer generally called the ECM. The computer receives information about the engine and other parts of the car from a system of sensors. This information is read by the computer several times a second. It is compared with the computer's memory and changes are made to the way the engine is running. If, for example, the throttle position and low vacuum readings tell the computer the engine is under a heavy load and accelerating, more fuel is fed to the fuel injectors and the engine timing is changed. The system works perfectly provided all the sensors, wiring, and the computer do their job. When one or more of the sensors provide readings that don't make sense to the computer, the yellow

check-engine light switches on and the computer ignores the
bad data from the errant sensor. You might drive your car
safely with the yellow warning light on, but make sure your
mechanic gets to the cause of the problem as soon as possible.
An ignored check-engine warning can be costly. When the
check-engine light is on, your fuel consumption will probably
be higher than normal. Check your owner's manual for specific details about the check-engine warning system on your
car. On some cars there is a "service soon" light and on
others the warning might read "power loss." It may also be
red.

Diagnoses and Solutions

One: At your earliest convenience, raise the hood and
check for any disconnected vacuum hoses at the carburetor
fuel injection. Secure these if you can. If not, have them
secured and the air filter checked to be sure it is not clogged
with dirt. Replace the air filter if it is dirty. Start the engine
and check to see if the yellow warning light stays off.

Two: Unlike the oil-pressure warning light or the temperature warning light, the check-engine light does not warn of
one specific problem. To determine where the problem is
located, your mechanic must ask your onboard computer
where it hurts. Generally this is better left to a mechanic who
has the training and electronic equipment required to check
for trouble codes or, as they are sometimes called, fault
codes. Once the mechanic has obtained the trouble codes,
he has an idea of where to look for the problem and has a
better estimate of what it will cost to repair the trouble once
it has been isolated.

Alternator Warning Light

Symptoms

Your car starts normally and you're driving down the road with not a care in the world. Suddenly a red warning light flashes on the instrument panel. The words *alternator, charge, alt*, or *battery* might be visible. Obviously there is a problem with the electrical system, no matter what you call the light. What you do next could make the difference between getting home quickly and being delayed several hours.

Explanation

When you operate the starter to start the engine, you are withdrawing electrical current out of the battery. As you run the engine, the alternator recharges the battery to replace the electrical current you withdrew from the battery when starting. If you keep running the starter without allowing the engine to run to recharge the battery, eventually the battery will go dead. If you start the engine and the alternator is not working properly, it will not recharge the battery. The electrical drain on the battery after the engine is running is only a fraction of the drain that occurs when the starter motor is running. In a properly working system, the alternator provides all of the electrical power needed to run the headlights, air conditioner, defroster, radio, lights, and so on. It also provides additional electrical current to recharge the battery. When the alternator is unable to recharge the battery, the battery must provide all of the power to keep the engine and the accessories running. For the charging system to work properly, the fuses, connections, belt, wiring, alternator, and regulator must be in good order. One break in this system will cause the battery to become discharged (see page 255).

Diagnoses and Solutions

One: The red charge light warns that the alternator is no longer doing its job of charging the battery. The battery has a certain amount of reserve capacity that will be enough to keep the engine running for about half an hour. Higher-capacity batteries will provide you with a little extra running time. So, from the moment the red charge light flashes, you probably have about half an hour to get to a place where you can safely shut off the engine. The key here is to keep the engine running. Shut off all unnecessary accessories. Turn off the air conditioner or heater. Shut off the radio and don't use the power windows and seats or anything else electrical. Also, don't pull off the road and shut off the engine so that you can look under the hood. Stopping won't help unless you happen to have a spare fuse, belt or alternator in the trunk along with the tools you will need to install them. Although you might have enough electrical power stored in the battery to keep the engine running, you will probably not have enough to restart the engine once you shut it off. If your regular mechanic is within half an hour's drive, go to him. If not, drive to the nearest mechanic for assistance (see page 255).

Two: If you are too far from your favorite mechanic, you could drive for about half an hour and then have your battery recharged at a local gas station. Once the battery is fully charged, you can run for another half hour, provided you don't keep restarting and use as few accessories as possible. Once you get to a mechanic, have the battery recharged, then tested, and have the alternator, regulator, belts, and fuses checked. Ask for a complete charging-system analysis.

Three: If you notice the temperature warning light eventually come on, it is most likely that a belt has broken. On many cars the same belt that drives the alternator also drives the water pump. If the temperature warning light comes on, you will need to pull off the road as soon as possible to keep the engine from overheating. If the belt is missing, twisted, or slipping, have your mechanic install a new belt and check the other belts for wear.

Brake Warning Light

Symptoms

The brakes feel perfectly normal or you detect a very slight difference in the feel of the brake pedal, but you are not alarmed. The red brake warning light flashes on the instrument panel. You assume it is the parking-brake warning light malfunctioning. You are not sure whether or not you actually have a problem. On some cars the brake warning light and the parking-brake light are one. Check your owner's manual to determine how your car works.

Explanation

Modern cars are equipped with a dual braking system. This means there is a separate hydraulic system for the front brakes and another for the rear. On some cars the split is between one front and one rear wheel in one system and the other front and rear wheel in another system. The idea is to make it possible for you to stop the car even if a leak develops at any point in the system. When the leak occurs and there is a sudden drop in brake-fluid pressure while braking, a special valve shuts off half the brake system. At the same time, it switches on the brake warning light. Never ignore the brake warning light. Even if it just flashes on occasionally, it is a possible sign of trouble brewing in the brake system. The system is only good for a limited time. When the warning light flashes make an appointment with your mechanic as soon as possible. You may be stopping with just two wheels. Left unrepaired, this could lead to total brake failure (see page 252).

Diagnoses and Solutions

One: On most cars with a separate warning light for the parking brake and the foot brake, you can quickly check for a problem by setting the parking brake. If the warning light that concerns you goes out when you release the parking brake, there is no serious problem. A parking-brake cable adjustment might be needed, or a rear brake lining replaced. If the brake warning light stays on, try lifting the parking-brake pedal or handle to see if the light goes off. If it does, the trouble might be with the parking-brake light switch, which is not a serious problem. Have the switch repaired or replaced at your earliest convenience.

Two: If the brake warning light stays on, you have a serious problem. It warns of a possible loss of brake fluid. Your first actions should be to slow down and get to the nearest service station. Once there, have the brake master cylinder fluid checked. If the master cylinder is low on fluid, have some DOT-approved brake fluid added and check to see if the light goes out. In most cases, even when the brake warning light is on, you will still have some braking power. You might have to press the brake pedal harder, and you will not stop as quickly, but you can generally get to safety if you drive slowly and remember to maintain a greater distance between you and the car ahead. Get your car to a mechanic as soon as possible for a complete brake check and repair. Ask your mechanic for an explanation of the leak.

Three: The brake warning light might also come on because the rear brakes are in need of adjustment. Don't just simply have the rear brakes adjusted. Have the front brake pads checked, and have the rear brake drums removed and the rear brakes inspected.

Oil-Pressure Warning Light

Symptoms

A persistent red warning light suddenly appears. The oil-pressure warning light is without doubt the most important warning light on your car's instrument panel. When the engine oil pressure drops, the problem is as serious for your engine as it would be if we were talking about your own blood pressure.

Explanation

Whenever engine oil pressure drops, the circulation of motor oil is reduced or even stopped. When this happens, there is a reduced flow of motor oil to the engine bearing surfaces. Whenever an engine runs it needs a flow of oil to the bearings. If the flow of oil is cut off or slowed, friction damage occurs to the surfaces of the bearings. In time, even if the oil pressure is restored, these tiny scars lead to bearing failure. If the engine oil pressure is not restored and the bearings run dry of oil, they very quickly overheat and actually melt. Once a bearing melts, the resulting damage to the engine is major. In some cases the entire engine must be replaced. The key to knowing just how far you can get when the oil-pressure light comes on is the sound of the engine. Any unusual engine noise such as rattling, knocking, or clicking warns of low oil pressure. Your safest course of action is to stop the engine as soon as possible and seek professional help. Not every mechanic is capable of diagnosing and repairing engine oil pressure problems. Before you agree to the repair, make sure the mechanic is experienced in this type of work. Ask for a written estimate including the cost of disassembly and testing. Find out what it will cost to reassemble the engine if you don't do the work.

Diagnoses and Solutions

One: Switch on your four-way emergency warning flashers and pull over to the slow lane. Slow down and pull off the road as soon as you can do so safely. Turn off the engine. Check the engine-oil dipstick. If the oil level is low or you cannot read any trace of oil on the dipstick, you first need to add motor oil. If you happen to have some motor oil in your trunk, add it to the engine and recheck the dipstick. In an emergency, any grade of motor oil will do, even a few quarts of transmission fluid. However, remember to change the oil as soon as possible if you use anything other than the specified type of oil. If adding motor oil causes the oil-pressure warning light to stay off, it is safe to drive your car to the nearest service station. Have the mechanic recheck the oil level and look for leaks. When an engine loses oil, there has to be a reason. Generally loss of motor oil means a leak. It might also mean the engine is worn and is burning the oil. If adding oil does not cause the oil-pressure warning light to go out, shut down the engine and call for a tow.

Two: In some instances the oil-pressure warning light will only go on when the engine is idling. If you find that the oil-pressure light flashes on at idle but goes out when the engine speed is increased, you should be able to drive to the nearest service station. Assuming the engine is full of oil, there is a problem with the oil pressure. The problem is usually a worn engine. When the engine bearings and oil pump wear, they allow a pressure loss. At idle, the engine turns more slowly and hence the oil pump is not pumping as hard as it would at higher engine speeds. Ask your mechanic to check the engine oil pressure. He will do this by installing a separate oil-pressure gauge to make sure the problem is actually low engine oil pressure and not a problem with the electrical wiring. If you must drive before you get your car to a mechanic for repairs, try adding a can of oil additive such as STP oil treatment. This won't repair a worn engine, but it might provide a little extra body to the oil and help keep the oil pressure up as the car idles.

Three: You might find that the engine oil-pressure light comes on only after a long drive, when the engine is fully warmed up. If this is the case, try allowing the engine to fully cool off. Restart and see if the engine oil-pressure light stays off. As long as the light is out, you can safely drive to the nearest service station. Should it flash back on, pull over and allow the engine to cool. Ask the mechanic to check for oil pressure loss. Make sure you're dealing with a mechanic competent to do major engine repairs.

CAUTION: Driving just a few miles with the oil-pressure light on could mean the difference between a major and minor repair expense. Take the warning seriously.

Engine-Temperature Warning Light

Symptoms

Your engine is running just fine, but suddenly a red warning light on your instrument panel flashes the words *Engine Temperature*. On some cars the words *Coolant Temperature* are used, or the more sophisticated engine warning system might say *Overheating*. What it all boils down to—pardon the pun—is that the mixture of antifreeze and water known as coolant is too hot and might even be boiling.

Explanation

A tremendous quantity of heat is generated each time a spark plug ignites the air-fuel mixture in its cylinder. Part of this heat goes out of the tailpipe with the exhaust, but a great deal of it has to be removed by the cooling system. To do this, coolant is pumped through small passages in the engine and around the cylinder walls. The heat from combustion in the cylinders is transferred to the metal walls of the engine. It is then transferred to the coolant flowing through the engine. This hot coolant is circulated by the water pump through the radiator, where the heat in the coolant is transferred to the air passing through the radiator. A loss of coolant interrupts this heat transfer and causes the remaining coolant to overheat and boil. If a fan belt turning the water pump breaks, the pump can no longer circulate coolant through the engine. The remaining coolant boils and the car overheats.

The same thing happens when a thermostat fails to open. The radiator, hoses, engine, and so on must be free of leaks and able to hold pressure. The average car runs at a cooling-system pressure of about 18 psi (pounds per square inch). To prevent the coolant from boiling, particularly on hot days, this pressure must be maintained. A worn radiator cap will release pressure and possibly cause overheating even if there are no other problems in the cooling system (see page 258).

Diagnoses and Solutions

One: The first thing you can do to alleviate an overheating condition is to switch on your car heater, even if it is the middle of summer. The heater helps cool off the engine coolant, but this is only a temporary measure. As soon as it is safe to do so, pull over to the slow lane and switch on your four-way emergency flashers. When you find a safe place to pull off the road, do so, but wait before you pop open the hood. Think about what you might expect to find there. If the engine is really overheating, there might be traces of steam vapor already coming out from under the car or through the grill.

> **CAUTION: Before you even try to open the hood, look under the engine. If you see a stream of engine coolant, you know you have a cooling-system leak from a hose, the radiator, the water pump, or perhaps a heater valve. Be careful here. Remember, there is really no rush to open the hood until the engine cools down on its own. Adding water or opening the hood is going to put you at risk. *Never* try to remove the radiator cap when the engine is hot. If you can't comfortably grasp the upper radiator hose, the engine is still too hot for you to safely remove the radiator cap. All modern engines are under pressure. When you remove the cap, chances are that hot coolant will gush out and possibly injure you or people standing nearby.**

Two: When the engine has fully cooled off and you can safely look under the hood, check for coolant in the recovery tank and in the radiator. See your owner's manual for the location of the recovery tank on your car. If either is empty, fill them with a mixture of half water and half antifreeze (see page 258). If nothing else is available in an emergency, you could use the water in your windshield-washer tank. Use plain water if you have to, and add the antifreeze when it is possible to do so. Look over the hoses to see if you can spot a hole. If you spot a small leak in a hose, try wrapping the hose with duct tape, adhesive tape, or even electrical tape. This won't hold up under pressure, but it might help get you home or to a service station. Reinstall the radiator cap, but instead of twisting it fully clockwise, as you would normally do, do not twist the cap. This will release any pressure buildup in the cooling system and reduce the leak. Ask your mechanic to pressure test the cooling system to find any leaks. Also check the operation of the thermostat and cooling fan.

Three: Overheating can also be caused by a loss of coolant from a leak in the radiator, a hole in a hose, a leaking heater, a leaking heater valve, a worn water pump, or a leaking gasket. You might not have any leak, however, and still have an overheating problem. If the overheating is accompanied by a loud rapping sound from the engine, the problem is very likely a defective thermostat. If the water-pump belt has broken or is slipping, the engine will overheat. If the radiator becomes clogged, the coolant can begin to boil. One frequently overlooked cause of overheating is the engine-fan clutch. The fan clutch attaches the engine fan to the engine. If it is worn and slipping, the engine fan might not be turning fast enough to cool the engine. A new fan clutch will be needed to correct this problem.

Four: On front-wheel-drive cars, the engine is cooled by a separate electric fan mounted on the radiator. If the electric fan does not switch on when the engine is fully warmed up, the engine will eventually overheat. On front-wheel-drive cars, after you have checked to be sure the radiator is full of coolant, check to be sure the radiator-cooling fan is working. In an emergency you can generally make the fan switch on by switching on the air conditioner. Normally, the fan will only switch on when the engine is quite warm. It might also run for a few minutes after you shut off the ignition switch. Ask your mechanic to check the fan motor, relay, fuses, and coolant temperature sensor for defects.

CAUTION: Always keep in mind that an engine's cooling system operates under pressure. With the radiator cap in place, a warmed-up engine might seem harmless when the ignition key is turned off. This is not true. Twisting off the radiator cap can send boiling coolant spraying out of the top of the radiator. Literally hundreds of people are injured each year because they removed the radiator cap before the engine cooled off. If the car is overheated, removing the radiator cap will not make it cool off any faster. In fact, it will probably cause further loss of coolant. Wait until you can comfortably grasp the upper radiator hose before you attempt to remove the radiator cap. One more important point: Don't assume that adding more antifreeze will make your car run better. Too much antifreeze does more harm than good. Generally a mixture of half antifreeze and half water is right for most cars. In colder climates you might want to have more antifreeze. Check your owner's manual or the chart available at most stores that sell antifreeze.

Antilock Warning Light

Symptoms

The antilock warning light on your instrument panel stays on after you have started the engine and the usual time for it to go out has elapsed, suddenly goes on and stays on as you are driving, or comes on when you depress the brake pedal. Whichever way it occurs, when the amber antilock warning light comes on, it signals trouble in your antilock-braking system. The antilock-brake system is generally referred to as ABS. Some cars do not have a separate ABS light. On these cars the ABS warning indicator is actually the same red warning light discussed under "Brake Warning Light" (page 73). Check your owner's manual to determine which warning-light system is used on your car.

Explanation

ABS brake systems are extremely complicated and there are several systems in use. Essentially, what an ABS system does is carefully monitor the speed of each wheel during braking. When one of the wheels locks up or spins faster than the others, the system takes over and pulses the brakes. This is really the action a professional driver would take in a skid. For this system to work, the sensors must constantly know what the wheels are doing. When a sensor is damaged or a wire is broken, the system cannot work. In addition, the system works under high pressures and, in most cases, is controlled by a computer. A mechanic who would attempt to diagnose and repair any ABS system must have the special equipment and knowledge needed for this highly technical system.

Diagnoses and Solutions

One: Check to see if you have forgotten to release the parking brake. The ABS system is designed to detect a wheel that is locking up. The term *wheel lockup* simply means that the wheel is no longer turning. It is locked by the brakes.

Two: Check the brake-fluid level in the master cylinder (see page 252). Low brake fluid generally means there is a leak somewhere in the system. Low brake fluid can also trigger the brake warning light. Be careful to refill your master cylinder with the brake fluid approved for your car. See page 254 for insight into the dos and don'ts of brake fluid.

Three: Have all four wheels removed and the condition of the brake pads and linings checked. Worn brake pads or linings might be the problem. In addition, the ABS warning sensors located at each of the wheels should be checked. If a sensor or the wire attached to it is damaged, the ABS warning light will turn on.

Air Bag Warning Light

Symptoms

Normally, turning the ignition key will cause several warning lights to be illuminated on the instrument panel. The air bag warning light should go on for a few moments, then turn off after the engine is running. On some cars there might be a warning light marked "Infl reset," which also pertains to the air bag system. See your owner's manual for the specific type of warning system used on your car.

Explanation

The air bag warning light is designed to alert you to a problem with the air bag system. On some cars there might also be a tone that alerts you to a problem with the air bag system. Most important of all is to check to make sure the air bag warning light comes on when you first turn the key.

Diagnoses and Solutions

One: If the air bag light goes on and stays on even after you have started the engine, try turning off the engine and waiting for a few seconds. Restart the engine and check the light. If it first goes on, then shuts off after you have started the engine, the system is working normally. Keep a watchful eye out for the air bag warning light the next several starts. Make sure, too, that the light first goes on, then turns out.

Two: If you observe that the air bag light never comes on, even when you first start the engine, you might have a serious problem with either the air bag system itself or the warning system. Read the owner's manual to determine how the air bag warning light should work on your car. On some cars the warning light will go on the moment the key is turned to the on position, then go off. A problem might exist if the warning light does not illuminate when you turn the key to the on position. You will need the help of a competent mechanic who has the equipment, literature, and skill to test and repair an air bag system. Don't trust this repair to just anyone. Make sure you are dealing with someone who actually knows the system and how it works.

CAUTION: If the air bag light does not go on, you have no assurance that the system is working. If, for example, the air bag warning light suddenly started flashing, there could be a problem in the system that would keep the air bag from deploying in the event of an accident.

Sounds, Smells, Smoke, and Leaks

Growling Sound from Front of Engine at Idle

Symptoms

This noise is more noticeable while the engine is running at idle. It is a growling, rotating noise. When you open the hood you hear it at the very front of the engine on rear-wheel-drive cars. On front-wheel-drive cars it is more likely to be near the right front fender. When you shut off the engine it stops immediately. When you race the engine it might be less noticeable.

Explanation

It is very easy to be confused by the sound of any one of the components driven by the same power source. It is wise to take extra time to check, or have your mechanic check, to be sure that the growling noise actually comes from the component it appears to be coming from. I have very often seen water pumps changed because the owner thought the noise came from the water pump when actually the noise was caused by the air pump or even a fan-belt idler pulley.

Diagnoses and Solutions

One: The water pump, power-steering, alternator, smog pump, and air-conditioner compressor are all driven by belts. These belts are rotated by the crankshaft pulley on most cars.

In that there is a common source of power, all of these components are driven at nearly the same speed. This makes it difficult to determine precisely which is the cause of the noise. To find the noise you have to go through a process of elimination. Start by listening for the noise with the air conditioner turned on, then try it with the air conditioner turned off. If the growling noise stops completely when the air conditioner is turned off, chances are the noise is in the air-conditioner compressor. Your mechanic will probably need to replace the air-conditioner compressor or the air-conditioner clutch, and may also need to recharge the refrigerant gas.

Two: Check the power-steering fluid reservoir—usually located on the power-steering pump—to be sure it is full of fluid (see page 248). Low fluid in the power-steering reservoir will cause a growling noise. It is usually more noticeable when the steering wheel is turned. Have your mechanic check the power-steering system for leaks, if a loss of fluid was detected.

Three: The water pump is located in the front of the engine on rear-wheel-drive cars. On front-wheel-drive cars it is to one side. On rear-wheel-drive cars the water pump can generally be found just behind the engine fan. It's easy to spot the fan because it looks like a fan you have at home to cool off in summer. Usually the fan is attached to the water pump with just a pulley separating the fan from the front of the water pump. When you suspect the noise is coming from the water pump, there is a simple way to check it. Make sure the engine is off. Remove the keys and disconnect the battery to be safe. Grasp the engine fan with two hands. If you can rock the fan easily so that the pulley has visible movement, the water-pump bearing is probably worn and causing the noise. Checking the pump is more difficult to do with front-wheel-drive cars because they generally have a separate electric fan attached to the back of the radiator and not attached to the pump. On many front-wheel-drive cars you can reach the water pump directly and rock it by hand to check for a worn bearing. This problem requires a mechanic. On some cars the water pump is under the timing belt cover and cannot easily be checked.

Four: Where the noise cannot easily be identified as a water pump, alternator, power-steering pump, smog pump, or compressor, the next step is to have a competent mechanic disconnect the belts to each of these components one by one. If the noise stops with the belt disconnected, he has found the source of the noise. Unless you're a terrific shade-tree mechanic this will probably require the service of a competent mechanic.

Growling Sound from Wheels When Moving

Symptoms

When you start moving forward at any speed above five miles per hour, you begin to hear a low-pitched growling or grinding sound. As you increase the car's speed, the noise becomes louder and faster. As you slow the car the sound slows. When you come to a stop, you no longer hear the sound. It begins again as the car rolls forward, gaining speed. It is important to know when the noise can be heard. A noise present when the car is not moving has an entirely different significance.

Explanation

For you to determine the cause of a growling or grinding noise, you must first determine when the noise occurs. If you hear the noise while the car is parked with the engine running, you can rule out the wheels, differentials, drive shaft, and tires as the source of the noise. When the car is parked, these parts of the car are not moving and cannot make a noise. Catching a noisy wheel bearing when it first starts making noise might limit the repair to just a new bearing. If left unrepaired, a noisy wheel bearing could destroy the housing or hub in which it rides. Replacing a wheel-bearing hub is expensive.

Diagnoses and Solutions

One: Put on an old pair of pants and get down on your hands and knees to check the tread surface of your tires for signs of wear. Look for sections where the tread rubber has worn so thin that the inner fabric is showing. Be extra careful to check for thin steel wires that might be protruding from a worn area of the tire. The steel wire in steel-belted radial tires can sometimes break through the worn spot, creating a sharp point waiting to puncture your fingers. Once you are sure there are no sharp wires sticking out of the tread, run your hand over the tire. It should be smooth and free of bumps. Bumps or flat spots in a tire will cause a low-pitched growling or grinding noise. The noise is similar to the noise a deep-cleated snow tire makes. Noisy tires cannot be repaired. Your only cure is to replace them.

Two: If the tires are free of bumps and flat spots, the noise is most likely related to a wheel bearing. It is generally easier to determine the source of the noise by driving on a quiet road with a smooth asphalt pavement. As you drive along, try to determine if the noise is from the front or rear of the car. Front-wheel bearing noises can sometimes be felt through the steering wheel. If you make a wide turn to the left, the left front wheel slows and the right front wheel speeds up. If the noise from the front of the car is louder on a left turn, you probably have a bad right front wheel bearing. If you suspect that the noise is from the rear of the car, have someone else drive while you sit in the backseat. First sit on one side, then the other. Place your hand on the floor and feel for the source of the noise. If you suspect the trouble is a wheel bearing, ask your mechanic to road-test the car with you. In the shop, your mechanic will have to try to isolate the offending wheel before he can accurately estimate the cost of repair.

Three: If the growling noise changes dramatically when you step on the gas, then changes again when you remove your foot, it might be caused by wear in the differential. Choose a mechanic who has experience in the diagnosis and repair of differentials. It is not a job for just any mechanic. Get a written estimate.

Four: If the growling noise suddenly changes or disappears when the transmission shifts into a higher gear, the problem is most likely in the transmission or transmission torque converter. Check the transmission dipstick for evidence of strong-smelling burnt transmission fluid. A noisy transmission or burnt transmission fluid (or both) usually indicates impending transmission failure. Start looking around for a competent transmission mechanic to rebuild your transmission in the very near future.

CAUTION: It is important to pay attention to new noises. Hearing a growling sound that alerts you to inspect your tires might save you from a dangerous tire blowout. Worse yet, a worn noisy bearing can seize, and that could put your car out of control at highway speeds.

Thumping Sound from Wheels When Moving

Symptoms

Driving forward, you hear a muffled thumping that corresponds to the rotation of the wheels. Moving slowly, you can almost hear each thump. As you drive faster, the thumping becomes more rapid. You might feel a slight movement in the steering wheel, which becomes more pronounced as you move ahead faster.

Explanation

Tire treads can flatten, bulge, or tear off with age. Any one of these conditions manifests itself as a thumping noise that occurs as the tire rotates. Check your tires often to spot any bulges, bumps, flat spots, or damaged tread, which could lead to a highway breakdown (see page 230).

Diagnoses and Solutions

One: A thumping sound most often indicates a tire problem. If this occurs while you're driving, slow down and pull to a safe area as soon as it is possible and safe to do so. You will have to get down on your hands and knees to carefully check all four tires. Drive the car forward about three feet so that you can check the area of the tires that had been contacting the ground. A large bulge in the area of the tread or protruding out of the sidewall will cause a thump as the bulging part of the tire hits the road surface. A tire bulge occurs when air gets between the layers of the tire. Install the spare tire as soon as possible, and replace the bulging tire as soon as possible.

> **CAUTION: A tire bulge or other serious defect is a dangerous condition and should not be ignored.**

Two: If you cannot detect a bulge in the tire tread or tire wall, the thumping might be caused by a more subtle flat spot or lump across the tread area. Be careful about protruding steel wires, which could injure your hand. Either jack up the car to free each wheel, or have your mechanic put the car on a lift. When the tire is rotated by hand, if there is a flat spot, you can generally spot it by looking at a fixed point with relation to the tire tread. As the tire rotates, the distance between the fixed point and the tire tread should remain the same. If the gap momentarily narrows as the tire is rotated, there might be a bulge in the tire. If the gap widens, there is a flat spot in the tire. Either way, you'll need to have the tire replaced.

Engine Rattles While Accelerating

Symptoms

One of the most common engine noises is a rattling sound heard when accelerating. It sounds as if someone had put half a dozen marbles in a metal pot and was shaking the pot. Some drivers have described the sound as if someone were rapidly tapping on the engine with a small hammer. This sound is generally known as a ping. You generally hear it when you step hard on the gas pedal going uphill.

Explanation

Pinging most often occurs when the mixture in the combustion chamber explodes before or after it should for efficient engine operation.

Diagnoses and Solutions

One: At some point, just about every car will develop a slight ping. When you hear a ping, try letting off the gas pedal a bit to see if it helps. Don't go rushing off to the mechanic just yet. Wait until your fuel has dropped down to near empty, then refill your tank with fuel from a reliable gas station. If the ping persists, check your owner's manual to make sure you are using the proper octane for your car. Although most cars will run well on the gas for which the engine was designed, some cars require higher-octane gas.

Two: When a ping persists, check for overheating. If a thermostat sticks or if there is a loss of pressure in the cooling system, an engine might run hotter and begin to ping. Have the source of the overheating diagnosed by a mechanic.

Three: Proper engine timing is critical in preventing ping. Older cars require that the timing be checked and adjusted to specification. An engine with incorrect timing can ping and also run hotter, which will contribute to the ping. Ask your

CAUTION: Pinging (detonation) can cause serious damage to engine pistons. The important thing is that you do not allow the engine to keep on pinging for any great length of time. Also, one of the more likely cures that will be offered to you is that you should use high-octane gasoline. Although this might stop the ping, it is an expensive cure. In some cases where engines have higher mileage, you will have no choice but to use higher octane. This should only be done once you are sure that no other cure will stop the ping. Higher-octane gasolines should only be used where specified in your owner's manual. Always use the octane recommended for your car in the manual. Some high-performance and luxury cars must have high-octane gasoline. Don't *guess*—check the owner's manual. Higher octanes are designed to reduce engine knock and have little, if any, effect on power (see pages 227, 238).

mechanic to check the timing. Modern computerized engines, when working properly, are automatically timed by the on-board computer and cannot be adjusted. On these engines detailed testing by a competent mechanic will be required to diagnose engine ping.

Four: Ping can also be the result of a vacuum hose or wire disconnected from an emission-control device; in particular,

a device known as the EGR valve. If all else fails, remind
your mechanic of the possibility that a ping might be caused
by a faulty or disconnected EGR valve.

Constant Tapping Noise from Engine

Symptoms

It is important when trying to determine the source of a
noise to listen carefully to the rhythm of the noise. In this
case, the tapping noise begins the moment the engine is
started and continues to some degree as long as the engine
is running. It will speed up as the engine rpms are increased
and slow down when the engine slows down. The constant
tapping can generally be heard loudest from the top of the
engine.

Explanation

Most of the fast tapping sounds from the top of an engine
are caused by a stuck hydraulic lifter. A hydraulic lifter is a
simple device designed to take up the normal expansion and
contraction that takes place during the heating and cooling
of metals. When one or more of the hydraulic lifters jam,
the slack that it normally would take up in the valve trains
remains. This causes a tapping sound.

Diagnoses and Solutions

One: If the sound lasts for just a short time when the
engine is cold, frequent oil changes might help free up the

lifter. If it persists, the lifter will have to be replaced to stop the noise. If your car is older, you may want to live with the noise, provided power is not reduced and no other performance problems exist.

Two: When the tapping sound is accompanied by a noticeable engine vibration at idle or a heavier vibration when the engine is put under a load, the likelihood is that one of the valve push rods or rocker arms has been broken. This is a sound that should not be ignored. To determine the cause, the rocker-arm covers will have to be removed by a mechanic so that the rocker arms, push rods, and valve stems can be seen. Very often this ominous-sounding noise can be repaired by simply replacing a rocker arm and bolt.

Three: In extreme cases, where the sound is present and there is also a muffled backfire that occurs when you accelerate, there might be damage to the engine camshaft. This is a major repair and should not be entered into without first getting a careful test of the camshaft to determine if the camshaft lobes are worn. If a camshaft is replaced, all of the hydraulic lifters should be replaced. This is also a good time to replace the timing chain or belt. Get an estimate of the cost of repairing the problem, and find out, before you leave the car, how much it will cost to reassemble the engine if you decline the work.

CAUTION: The tapping of a worn hydraulic lifter, broken rocker arm, or broken push rod should not be ignored. Find out what is causing the noise and what it will cost to repair it. Although it is true that a single noisy hydraulic lifter will not be too much of a problem, a broken push rod or rocker arm will cause gas waste, poor performance, and a loss of power, along with high emissions.

Heavy Knocking Sound from Engine

Symptoms

With the engine running, you hear a low-pitched banging sound from the engine. It might not be too apparent with the engine idling, but when you accelerate the knocking becomes louder and faster. It is a fast banging sound that might seem as if someone were rapidly pounding the side of the engine with a sledgehammer. Keep in mind this is a low-pitched sound that is best described as a banging rather than a tapping.

Explanation

As each cylinder fires its mixture of gasoline and air during the combustion stroke, a tremendous force is exerted on the piston. That force is transmitted through the connecting rod to the crankshaft. The only thing between the crankshaft and the connecting rod is a thin bearing. Through wear or a lack of oil, the bearing wears to a point where it allows the connecting rod to move more than it should. In some cases, this permits the piston to hit the cylinder head. In other cases the noise occurs when the extra space between the connecting rod and the piston is suddenly taken up. The banging noise you hear when the engine is run faster than idle is the piston pounding away at the delicate bearing surfaces of the crankshaft and connecting rods.

Diagnoses and Solutions

One: Before you do another thing, stop the engine and check the oil level. This type of engine banging sound very often results from running the engine without oil. The idea of checking the oil is to prevent any further damage. However, by the time the banging can be heard, there is already sufficient damage to warrant major repair. Here is how you can know for sure if that repair is needed. Set the parking brake and put the shift selector in park. Raise the hood and start the engine. Stand to the side of the car near the front fender so that you can easily hear engine noises. Have a friend step on the gas pedal to race the engine with the transmission still in park. If the knocking sound gets louder and faster as you raise the engine rpms, chances are the noise is caused by worn engine bearings. See a mechanic.

Two: A scraping sound in addition to the knocking sound indicates that the problem of worn engine bearings has progressed to the point where the bearings are so badly worn that immediate engine lock up is a real possibility. Driving the car is a real gamble. If there is any hope of saving the engine block it would be wise to have the car towed to a mechanic. Get an estimate for repairs and for reassembly if you don't accept the estimate.

CAUTION: The longer you wait to repair this noise, the more costly the repair. If you wait too long, the engine can be destroyed beyond repair. Either way, the noise is a warning that major engine repairs are needed. It also warns that the engine might seize at any moment.

Humming Sound from Under Car

Symptoms

The sound of your car moving forward gradually becomes louder and more noticeable. After a while you notice a definite growl or whine that seems to change when you accelerate or decelerate. The origin of the sound on a rear-wheel-drive car seems to be from under the rear passenger seats. On a front-wheel-drive car the noise seems to be coming from just under your feet. The sound might disappear entirely when you decelerate and become very noticeable when you are accelerating.

Explanation

The differential is the device that converts the rotating power of the drive shaft on a rear-wheel-drive car into the power that goes to both rear axles. It also adds a set of reduction gears which make the power delivered to the rear wheels greater than it would be if there were no gear reduction. Most important of all, the differential makes it possible for one rear wheel to turn faster than the other. If there were no differential, making a turn would cause the rear tires on a rear-wheel-drive car to skip and screech. On a front-wheel-drive car you would find it very hard to make a turn if there were no differential. One of the most characteristic noises caused by a worn differential is a humming sound. (You may have already heard it while riding in an older taxicab.)

Diagnoses and Solutions

One: If the sound you are hearing fits the description under Symptoms, check the differential fluid first. On a rear-wheel-drive car, the differential is located in the rear of the car in the center of the rear axle housing. The drive shaft connects to the differential. Even if you have just changed your motor oil or transmission fluid, it is possible for the differential to be dry of lubricant. If the pinion seal leaks or the differential cover gaskets leak, the vital lubricant will leak out. Running without lubricant will damage the differential. In an extreme case, the steel gear in the differential will actually melt and self-destruct. Front-wheel-drive cars also have differentials, but they are generally attached to the transmission to form what is known as the transaxle. Check your owner's manual to see if the differential on your front-wheel-drive car shares its lubrication with the transmission or if it needs to be refilled separately.

Two: If the differential is not low on lubricant, there might be worn gears or bearings that are causing the noise. Repairing the differential can be expensive and should not be attempted by anyone without a first-hand knowledge of how the differential works and how it must be installed.

Three: A noise similar to that made by a worn differential can be caused by a worn rear axle or front drive-axle bearings. An experienced mechanic might be able to sound out a worn rear axle bearing or front drive-axle bearing, but there is always the chance that a rear axle bearing or a front drive-axle bearing will make the same sound as a worn differential. If there is any serious doubt about which to replace first, choose the cheaper axle bearings.

> **CAUTION:** Before you agree to replacing axle bearings or to differential repairs, carefully check the tire treads on all four tires. A bumpy tire tread can make a noise that could be confused with a worn bearing.

Roaring Noise from Under Car

Symptoms

Your first inkling of a problem might have come when, backing out the driveway, you noticed the sound of your car echoing off the nearby wall of your house was somehow much louder; or perhaps you were driving along and suddenly you heard what has become a constant roaring. The sound is louder when the car is in gear and you accelerate. In neutral it might be only slightly louder than before the roar appeared.

Explanation

The exhaust system consists of a system of pipes and mufflers designed to safely carry the hot, poisonous exhaust gases from the engine safely past the underside of the car and out past the rear bumper. In addition, the exhaust system quiets or muffles the sound of the exhaust, hence the term muffler. Most cars have a steel exhaust system, which eventually rusts and breaks. Some newer cars have stainless-steel mufflers and pipes, which can be expected to last a great deal longer. Just after the pipe leading from the engine there is a device that looks like a muffler but is actually a catalytic converter. This device is designed to create a chemical reaction that will clean up the exhaust gases from your engine. It is an important part of the emissions-control system on your car and should not be removed. In fact, it is a violation of federal and state emissions laws to remove the catalytic converter (see page 264).

Diagnoses and Solutions

One: A sudden roar from under the car is more than likely caused by an exhaust-system leak. You can hear the noise better if you have someone momentarily accelerate the engine as you kneel down at the side of the car and look underneath. While you're kneeling down to hear the noise, look for any exhaust pipes or mufflers that might have dropped down. When a muffler or tailpipe breaks, a part of the pipe or muffler itself can drop down to where it is nearly touching the ground. If the pipe or muffler has dropped, there is the risk that it will touch the ground. When this happens the muffler or pipe can snag on the ground and twist up to jam under the car. The risk is that the muffler or pipe will damage a tire, cut a brake hose, or jam between the tire and the wheel well. If possible, tie a rope so that it will lift the muffler or pipe off the ground just enough so that you can slowly drive to a repair shop.

Two: Very often the exhaust will begin to make noise without there being any obvious broken pipe or muffler. A rust hole can suddenly blow out of the bottom of a muffler. The area where the tailpipe is welded to the muffler can also rust out, or the pipe itself might be rusted away. Where the exhaust leak is less obvious, you will have to have the car put on a lift for an exhaust inspection. Have the offending part or parts replaced.

Three: Where no obvious leaks in the exhaust pipes or mufflers can be found, yet the noise persists, have a mechanic check for possible exhaust-manifold leaks. A broken exhaust-manifold gasket or a cracked exhaust manifold will cause a similar noise. Have your mechanic determine the source of the leak and estimate the cost of repair. If the manifold is cracked you'll need a new one.

Four: Many emissions-control systems are tied into the exhaust system. Often they are vulnerable to rusting because of the heat and corrosive nature of exhaust gases. If the noise is coming from the front of the car and the exhaust system is in good condition, have a mechanic check for a break in one of the emissions tubes used to pump fresh air from the smog pump into the exhaust manifold or catalytic converter.

CAUTION: Use extreme caution when checking your exhaust system. The exhaust system can become very hot very quickly and could cause a serious burn if you grasp a pipe or muffler. The catalytic converter becomes especially hot and should never be touched unless you are absolutely sure it is cool. One other word on the catalytic converter: There is actually a very hot chemical process going on inside the converter. When additional fuel is run through the catalytic converter, as is the case when you're first starting the engine on a cold day, the catalytic converter can become extremely hot—so hot that dried grass or leaves under the car could ignite. For that reason, never park your car on a pile of leaves, in tall grass, or where there is a chance that any inflammable material could touch the catalytic converter.

Chirping Sound Under Car When Moving Slowly

Symptoms

You might first hear it when backing your rear-wheel-drive car out of the driveway; or you might hear it when you accelerate slowly on a quiet street. Either way, it's a squeaking, chirping sound that seems to get faster as you increase the car's speed. It stops the moment you stop the car, and you probably don't hear it at highway speeds.

Explanation

There are different types of drive shafts used on various models. Some have simple universal joints, whereas others use a more complicated constant-velocity joint. Some drive shafts have center-support bearings, which can wear and cause a vibration. The noise you hear is a worn joint.

Diagnoses and Solutions

One: The first place to look when you hear a fast chirping sound coming from under a rear-wheel-drive car is at the universal joints. The universal joints allow the drive shaft to move up and down without breaking. Each universal joint has four or more bearings. When these bearings dry out and rust, the first symptom is a chirping sound that increases as the drive-shaft speed increases. See a mechanic as soon as possible.

CAUTION: Left unrepaired, a noisy universal-joint bearing will eventually wear out and can allow the drive shaft to drop out of the car.

Two: When the universal joints wear to a point where they allow the drive shaft to run off-center, you might also feel a vibration or rumble coming from the center of the car under the seats. What is happening is that the worn bearings or universal-joint yoke allow the drive shaft to vibrate. A damaged drive shaft can also cause this type of vibration. See a mechanic as soon as possible. If you're a long way from your favorite mechanic, you may want to have the car towed. Avoid high speeds.

Clicking Ratchet Sound on Turns (Front-Wheel Drive)

Symptoms

As you accelerate slowly into a U-turn, you feel a muffled click or ratcheting sound coming from either the right or left front wheel, or both, on your front-wheel-drive car. When you drive straight ahead, the sound seems to disappear but recurs nearly every time you make a sharp turn.

Explanation

The clicking ratchet sound of a worn front-wheel drive-axle joint is unique to front-wheel-drive cars. CV joints are covered with a soft rubber that has probably torn and allowed the lubricating grease to be washed out of the joint.

Diagnoses and Solutions

One: Don't panic and pull off to the side of the road. What you're probably hearing is a worn front drive-axle constant-velocity (CV) joint. As soon as possible, have your mechanic check the front drive axles. In some cases replacing the torn drive-axle boots and installing the special grease used for these joints will stop the noise, provided the joints are not already too far worn. If they are rusty or damaged, they need to be replaced by a competent mechanic.

Two: Rusty or damaged CV joints can be repaired either by installing new CV joints or a new or remanufactured front drive-axle assembly.

CAUTION: Noisy CV joints are not a problem that should be ignored, despite the fact that you might have been driving around with the noise for several months. Eventually the joint will be so severely damaged that it may come apart and allow the front drive axle to come apart and cause a breakdown.

Exhaust Sound at Tailpipe Uneven or "Out of Tune"

Symptoms

You have grown used to the even hum of the exhaust gases coming out of the tailpipe as the engine idles. It has always been an even, smooth tone. One day you notice that the noise from the tailpipe is no longer an even tone. It is more of a rhythmic sound, where the tone changes rapidly. From a long, constant *broooom* sound it begins to sound more like *roooom, rooom, room*. In other words, you detect an uneven sound in the exhaust at the tailpipe.

Explanation

This condition could be caused by something as simple as a bad spark plug, or it could be the result of a worn valve or piston ring. Every internal combustion engine is designed to work as a unit. The power contributed by each cylinder must be the same and in balance. When any part of the engine malfunctions, the engine might still run, but its overall performance is diminished. One of the ways a motorist can be alerted to a developing problem is by a change in the sound of the engine or a loss of power. See page 235 for a further explanation of cylinder-power balance.

Diagnoses and Solutions

One: There is a very definite tone to every car's exhaust system. When there is a sudden change in the even tone you are used to hearing at idle, chances are that one of the cylinders is no longer firing or not firing properly. First have a mechanic check for worn spark plugs, shorted ignition wires, or a faulty distributor cap or rotor.

Two: If the ignition system is okay, the next thing to do would be to have a computerized engine-analysis done. This will double-check the ignition system, point out any weak cylinders, and also explore the possibility of a fuel-delivery problem that could be causing one or more cylinders to not function properly.

Fluid Leaking Under Car
(Oily and Black)

Symptoms

As you pull into your driveway, you notice some evidence of an oil leak in the spot where you parked your car the night before. It might start with a few drops of black oil on the ground under the front of the car. Then you start to notice larger and larger spots of black oil. You become really alarmed when you see a small pool of black oil about the size of a silver dollar.

Explanation

It is very important to make checking fluid levels a regular part of caring for your car. Whether you do it yourself or have your mechanic do it, make sure it is done at the very least once a month. Any sudden loss of fluid can tip you off to trouble about to happen. Let's say, for example, your transmission develops a leak. Long before you have lost enough fluid for you to notice a slip in the transmission, the transmission-fluid level will have dropped to where it will show on the transmission-fluid dipstick. If you don't check the transmission fluid and a leak develops, the fluid will leak out until there isn't enough fluid in the transmission. When this happens, air is sucked up into the fluid and the hydraulic components in the transmission malfunction (see page 207).

Diagnoses and Solutions

One: Check the engine-oil dipstick to be sure your engine is not too low on oil to safely run. If the oil cannot be measured on the dipstick, add oil before running the engine. If the oil level is at the "Add oil" mark, drive to the nearest service station for oil. If it takes two or three quarts of oil to bring the engine-oil level up to where it belongs, you either have a serious leak or you haven't checked the oil level for too long a time. If the latter is the case, and you can't remember when you last checked the oil, shame on you. Now that you feel guilty because you have neglected to check the oil, you have to make it your business to check the oil every day for the next week. If you find that your oil is getting lower every day, make an appointment to have your mechanic put the car on a lift to check the engine for oil leaks. If, on the other hand, you have been good about checking your oil and you know that there is a sudden drop in the engine-oil level, you can be pretty certain a leak has developed.

Two: Let's assume you know you have an oil leak but

aren't sure if it is from the engine, transmission, or power-steering system. The best way to determine where a leak is coming from is to carefully check the engine oil, transmission oil, and power-steering fluid levels every day for a week to see which is dropping. Heavy leaks will show up very quickly using this method. Smaller leaks or seepage will be more difficult to pinpoint. See a mechanic for repair and let him know which source you suspect.

Three: Use a sheet of newspaper or, better yet, a large piece of cardboard. White cardboard works the best. At night, after you park the car, put the newspaper or cardboard under the car in the area where you saw the leaks. If there are still some spots of oil on the ground, use several layers of newspaper to keep what is on the ground from soaking through. Weigh the paper down with some rocks if you think the wind might blow the paper away. The next morning, pull the paper out from under the car. Next, remove the engine-oil dipstick and splash a few drops of the oil on the dipstick onto the newspaper. Do the same with the transmission-oil dipstick. Now compare the two samples you took from the dipsticks to the oil spots on the newspaper that dripped out from under the car. You will notice the engine oil is black. The transmission fluid will be dark red or dark brown. On some cars the transmission fluid might be a dark green. If the sample on the paper does not exactly match either the transmission or engine dipstick samples, compare the spots with a sample of the fluid from the power-steering dipstick. If you're having difficulty figuring out which sample matches better, bring the newspaper to your mechanic and remember to tell him which fluid you have been adding.

> **CAUTION: A car might still run with low or empty fluid reservoirs, but damage will occur. The transmission clutch plates will start to overheat and the transmission will eventually fail. It is therefore extremely important to check all fluid levels often.**

Fluid Leaking Under Car (Oily and Red)

Symptoms

As you back out of the driveway or when you return at night to the spot where you parked your car the night before, you notice a spot of fluid that is not black like engine oil. Transmission fluid on most cars is a dark red. On cars with worn transmissions it might be a dark brown. On some newer cars the transmission fluid is a dark green.

Explanation

Your automatic transmission operates on hydraulic fluid pressure. Hydraulic fluid is pumped up to a high pressure, then sprayed against fins in the torque converter to transmit engine power to the transmission. Within the transmission, hydraulic pressure operates the clutches, valves, and servos that make your transmission work. When the transmission fluid leaks out, the fluid level drops. This causes the transmission hydraulic pumps to pick up air as well as fluid. Air in the transmission fluid will cause the transmission to slip. Slippage further damages the transmission.

Diagnoses and Solutions

One: Whenever you suspect a leak, always check both the engine-oil level and the transmission-oil level. When checking the transmission oil, follow the instructions printed in your owner's manual. On most cars with automatic transmissions, the oil must be checked with the engine running and the transmission in park. Learn how to read the transmission-oil dipstick. Remember to remove the dipstick, wipe it off with a clean cloth or paper towel, and then reinstall the stick to take the reading. It is nearly as bad to overfill the transmission as it is to not have enough fluid. Examine the markings on the transmission dipstick before you install it for the fluid-level test. When you add oil, check the level periodically and stop adding when the dipstick reading is in the "Full" range.

Two: If you have been careful about frequently checking your transmission-fluid level, a sudden low fluid reading on the transmission dipstick will tip you off to a leak. If you have been careless about checking the transmission fluid, you will have no way of knowing if the leak is a slow leak over time or one that has suddenly occurred. Either way, fill the transmission to the full mark and make a vow to Saint Vinny, the patron saint of auto mechanics, that you will mend your wicked ways and check your car's fluid levels often. If you find that you often need to keep adding transmission fluid to keep the level where it belongs, it is time to take the car to your mechanic for a check to see if the transmission seals or the transmission-pan gasket are leaking. While you're at it, ask your mechanic to check the transmission-cooler lines for leaks.

> **CAUTION: Running your transmission with less than the required amount of transmission fluid will cause costly damage.**

Fluid Leaking Under Car
(Yellow or Green)

Symptoms

It might be just a few drops of oil or some other fluid under the car, but whatever it is, it grabs your attention. In this case the fluid is either yellow or green and might appear oily, but not as oily as motor oil or transmission fluid.

Explanation

A cooling system runs on pressure to make the cooling process more efficient and to allow the coolant to run above the boiling point at which it would boil if it were not pressurized (see page 258). The modern automotive cooling system transfers a great deal of heat from the engine cylinders in a very short period. To do this efficiently, the coolant level must be kept full at all times. It is as important to check the coolant level as it is to check the motor oil and transmission fluid.

Diagnoses and Solutions

One: Drops or spots of yellow or green liquid under your car usually mean there is a coolant leak. Coolant, as you know, is the mixture of water and antifreeze that is poured into the radiator and circulates through the engine to keep it cool. When you see evidence of a coolant leak, raise the hood and check the coolant-recovery tank. The coolant-recovery tank is usually a semitransparent white plastic tank attached to either the right or left inner fender or to the right or left of the radiator. Many coolant-recovery tanks have the markings "hot" and "cold" molded into the side. Some have the word *coolant* printed on the cap. The important thing is that you know the difference between the coolant-recovery tank and the windshield-washer fluid tank. They look similar and in some cases are actually part of the same container. If you aren't sure, there is one foolproof way to know which is which. Look for a small black rubber hose, about half an inch in diameter, attached to the place where the radiator cap screws onto the top of the radiator. Follow that hose to the coolant-recovery tank. If the coolant-recovery tank is empty, chances are there is a coolant leak. You will next have to check for coolant in the radiator. Have your mechanic pressure test the cooling system to locate the leak. If you want to try to find the leak yourself, read on.

> **CAUTION: Do not even think about removing the radiator cap until the engine is cool and the pressure in the cooling system has dropped. When the engine is running, and for a long time after it is shut off, the cooling system will hold a pressure. If you release the cap while the coolant is still hot, you risk a serious burn, so don't try it.**

Two: Once you have determined the coolant level in the coolant-recovery tank and/or the radiator is low, you know for sure there has to be a leak somewhere. Start your search for a leak by checking the top of the engine for watery evidence of coolant leaking. If there is a pool of green or yellow coolant on top of the engine, check for a leaking heater or radiator hose. You will see wet spots and possibly steam vapor. A leaking thermostat gasket might also cause this type of coolant accumulation. Add a mixture of half water and half antifreeze to the radiator (see page 258). If there is a split hose you will see the coolant leak out soon after you fill the radiator. If you see no evidence of a leak on top of the engine, look under the engine after you have added coolant. A fast drip at the front of the engine might be an indication of a leak in the lower radiator hose or the water pump. A leak under the engine could be an engine core plug leaking. A leak under the radiator points you to the radiator. Generally, when the radiator is leaking you will see the trail of coolant leading to the point of the leak. If it is a very slow leak, the trail might leave a greenish powdery accumulation.

Three: Coolant leaks that aren't visible might require that the cooling system be pressurized, which is very often the only efficient way to find a coolant leak. This will require a mechanic. A leak that does not show at all might turn into a stream of coolant from the point of the leak once the system is under pressure. It is essential that the entire radiator be checked when looking for a leak. While the pressure is on, the mechanic should also look under the engine for leaks.

Four: If the coolant leak cannot easily be spotted with the system under pressure, there are some less obvious areas of potential leakage that should be considered. Very often a water pump that is leaking will not leak under a pressure test. In some cases the fluid leaks from a small hole (weep hole) on the underside of the water pump. Oddly, even if the pressure is maintained in the cooling system, the pump might not leak. For this type of problem, the best test is to carefully examine the weep hole at the base of the water pump. If there are telltale signs of coolant that reappear at the weep hole, there is more than likely a worn water-pump seal.

Yet another hard-to-find leak is from the heater core. To find this type of leak, you might have to remove part of the carpet under the heater to check for drops of coolant. Also, have a mechanic check the air conditioner drain hose. If there are droplets of green or yellow coolant in the drain hose, there is evidence of a heater-core leak. Have the mechanic also look at engine core plugs for droplets of coolant. Slow coolant leaks could be coming from the cylinder-head gaskets, thermostat gasket, any one of a dozen core plugs, loose bolts, the radiator itself, or any one of the hoses.

Fluid Leaking Under Car (Clear)

Symptoms

You notice a clear liquid accumulating on the ground under your car. Most often the watery-looking liquid will appear on the passenger side just to the rear of the right front tire. Or you might see an accumulation, on the driver's side, of a clear but more oily-looking liquid. This clear liquid may also appear at each of the wheels and in other places under the car.

Explanation

Drivers often forget that the air conditioner on any car removes moisture from the passenger compartment air as the air flows through. This water or condensate drips out of the air conditioner's drain tube, generally located on the passenger side behind the right front tire and just below the air-conditioner assembly. On most cars you can find the assembly bolted to the right side of the bulkhead under the hood. See page 262 for more information about how your air conditioner works.

Diagnoses and Solutions

One: When your air conditioner is working, particularly on a hot, humid day, it is perfectly normal for clear water to pour out of the air conditioner's drain tube. If this drain tube is not allowed to function properly, the water will pour into the passenger compartment floor and cause a mildewy odor.

Two: What appears to be clear water may actually be windshield-washer solvent. If the container leaks the solvent may puddle under the car. This might also occur when there is a leak in one of the hoses to the windshield-washer pump. To find the leak, fill the windshield-washer container and check under the car for leaks. You may need a new container, hose, or hose clamp.

Three: Brake fluid is clear in color but oily in texture. If the leak you noticed is near one of the wheels, just below the driver in the area below the brake pedal, you may have a brake-fluid leak. This clear liquid will not evaporate as quickly as plain water. Touch it with your fingers. If it is oily, it is probably brake fluid. Check the brake master-cylinder reservoir to see if there is a loss of fluid. Ask your mechanic to check the brake hydraulic system for leaks (see page 115).

CAUTION: Brake-fluid leaks should never be ignored. If there is a leak or a wet spot make sure you have a mechanic check it out and repair the leak before it leads to a brake failure. Air-conditioner condensate should be clear. If it has a greenish or yellowish color there may be a heater core leak.

Black Smoke from the Tailpipe

Symptoms

You might first be alerted to the presence of black smoke from the tailpipe by a black spot of soot on the driveway or against the back wall of your garage; or you might see a cloud of black smoke when you first start. When the condition is really extreme, you will see a constant stream of black smoke from the tailpipe. If you have been checking the gas mileage, you will have also noted that you're burning a great deal more gas per mile than you should.

Explanation

When an engine is cold, as it would be during starting, the gasoline does not easily vaporize; thus, the engine needs more gasoline to provide enough vapor for combustion to occur. On a carbureted engine, the choke valve closes to cause more fuel to be drawn through the carburetor. Mechanics call the mixture of air and fuel that flows through the carburetor and into the cylinders rich when there is more gasoline that normal. They call it lean when there is less gasoline than normal. When the choke is closed the mixture is rich to provide easy starting. Once the engine starts it quickly warms up, making the rich mixture for starting unnecessary. If the choke fails to open the mixture remains rich, and clouds of black smoke come out of the tailpipe. This same rich mixture collects on the spark plugs and causes them to foul. Fouling means that the tip of the spark plug becomes coated with the same black soot you see coming out of the tailpipe. The plugs might also actually become wet with gasoline. The result is that the spark plugs cannot do their job of presenting a spark in the cylinders to ignite the fuel-air mixture. This causes the engine to misfire. Stalling and no-starts will soon follow. The same thing happens on a car with fuel injection, but not because the choke stays closed, simply because there is no choke on a car with fuel injection.

The air-fuel mixture is made richer for starting by the computer, which receives signals from both the engine coolant-temperature sensor and the engine air-temperature sensor. These sensors advise the computer if the engine is warm or cold. When a sensor malfunctions, it may be telling the computer that the engine is cold when it is fully warmed up. This faulty sensor advisory could cause the computer to make the air-fuel mix richer when it should actually be leaner. The result is a rich mixture, spark-plug fouling, and black smoke.

A faulty oxygen sensor could do the same thing. If the oxygen sensor located in the exhaust system malfunctions, it could send a false message to the computer, causing a rich mixture. Extreme cases result in black smoke. Less serious problems result in decreased gas mileage and poor performance. The possibility of an overly rich mixture underscores the importance of having the emissions tested whenever your car is tuned up (see pages 234, 238, 267).

Diagnoses and Solutions

One: When you see black smoke from the tailpipe on a car equipped with a carburetor, the first thing to do is check for a clogged air filter (see page 241). Next, take a look at the automatic choke. When the engine is cold, the choke valve on top of the carburetor (see page 241) should be closed. It opens gradually as the engine warms up. If the choke valve stays closed even after the engine is warm, there will be too much fuel entering the combustion chamber. You can check this by removing the air filter (see page 241) when the engine is cold and observing the position of the choke valve. It should be closed when the engine is cold. On most cars you will have to gently tap the gas pedal to release the choke; do this without starting the engine. Reinstall the air filter, start the engine, and allow it to warm up. Once the engine is warm, shut it off. Remove the air filter and look again at the choke valve. It should now be in the open position. If it is not, you will need a repair to the choke mechanism. Very often a spray of carburetor cleaner will free up the choke. If you are a do-it-yourselfer, you might want to try this before you take the car to a mechanic.

Two: If you are on the highway and find that the choke is staying closed even after warming up, as an emergency measure you can put a screwdriver into the choke valve to keep it open long enough for you to get home. Ask your mechanic to check and repair the choke mechanism.

CAUTION: Be sure the screwdriver is large enough that it will not slip into the carburetor. Any foreign object in the carburetor can cause major engine damage.

Three: If your car is equipped with fuel injection, there is very little you can do to correct the black smoke condition even temporarily. About the only thing you can do is check for a clogged air filter. Beyond that you will need the help of a mechanic trained in fuel-injection diagnosis. Black smoke on these systems might be caused by a leaking fuel injector, or a faulty computer, oxygen sensor, temperature sensor, and so on.

Light Blue Smoke from the Tailpipe

Symptoms

When you first start the engine, you notice a cloud of light blue smoke from the tailpipe. After a few minutes it dies down and there might be no more smoke until you restart or until after the car has remained idle overnight; or you might notice that whenever you accelerate there is suddenly a cloud of blue behind you. After a while the blue smoke might be present whenever the engine is running.

Explanation

Light blue smoke from the tailpipe is caused by oil getting into the air-and-fuel mixture. This can happen in several ways and generally means a major repair. (See Diagnoses and Solutions for explanations of the possible causes.) It is a good idea to routinely check the tailpipe to observe the color of the exhaust. Generally you won't see the exhaust. On a cold or damp day, you might see some steam vapor, which quickly disappears. When you notice the exhaust has taken on a definite color, it is time to have your engine checked.

Diagnoses and Solutions

One: There is some hope on some cars for which the transmission is equipped with a vacuum-operated modulator. In some cases blue oil coming from the tailpipe might be caused by transmission fluid leaking from the transmission modulator and being drawn up through the transmission modulator vacuum hose into the engine. In this case the transmission will eventually become low on fluid. It takes only a slight leak to create blue smoke. Ask your mechanic to check for a leaking modulator and replace it if needed.

Two: If the blue smoke occurs only for a few moments when you first start the engine, there is the possibility that the engine-oil return holes in the cylinder heads are clogged. This causes the oil to pool and be drawn around the valve stems. To check for this condition, a mechanic would have to remove the valve rocker-arm cover or covers and check the oil returns.

Three: The next most likely cause of blue smoke is worn valve seals. The valve seals are little rubber seals that keep the motor oil from being drawn down between the engine valve and the hole in the cylinder head into which the valves are fitted. When the valve seals wear out, oil can be drawn into the engine intake manifold. Here, too, the mechanic must remove the valve rocker-arm cover to reach the valve seals. It is a more involved job than simply checking for a clogged oil return. In extreme cases the valve guide or hole in the cylinder head might be worn, allowing too much space between the valve stem and the valve guide hole. This allows oil to leak into the air-fuel mixture and be burned in the cylinders. The presence of oil in the cylinder might result in the fouling of one or more spark plugs. If the spark plugs frequently need to be cleaned because they have become wet with motor oil, you have a good indication of an internal engine-oil leak. All of these conditions require repair by a mechanic.

Four: Worn piston rings also allow motor oil to be drawn into the combustion chamber and burnt with the air and fuel. Generally, but not always, worn piston rings will cause lowered compression. A computerized engine analysis should be a part of every tuneup. It is the best way to discover a cylinder with low compression before it becomes a major problem.

White Smoke from the Tailpipe

Symptoms

You might have experienced a bout with engine over-heating or just noticed that you frequently have to add water and antifreeze to the coolant-recovery tank or radiator. Although you might have seen white vapor from the tailpipe before on a cold or rainy day, this now seems more than usual.

Explanation

When an engine is assembled, gaskets are placed between parts such as the engine cylinder head and the engine block. These gaskets are like the ham in a ham sandwich, with the cylinder head and block being the bread. The gasket provides an air- and water-tight seal between the cylinder head and the engine block. When that seal begins to leak, the pressure of the combustion occurring in each cylinder can push air and fuel into the cooling system. During the intake stroke, a vacuum is created in the cylinder, which sucks coolant into the cylinder. This results in a high pressure in the radiator and cooling system, then a loss of coolant as it is sucked into the cylinder. Before long the engine will overheat.

Diagnoses and Solutions

One: It is normal for there to be a short period of white smoke or steam vapor present at the tailpipe when you first start up. However, when it remains and seems to get heavier,

> **CAUTION:** Your engine cannot long survive an internal coolant leak. If it is only a leaking cylinder-head gasket, the repair is fairly inexpensive. If left unrepaired, it can lead to overheating, which could damage the cylinder heads or even cause a crack in the engine block. The latter is an extremely expensive repair (see page 258).

there might be a problem. Perhaps the best indication of a problem is the presence of a sweet smell in the white smoke that you don't normally smell when you start your car. This might be the early signs of an internal engine-coolant leak. This generally means a leaking cylinder-head gasket; or it might be more serious: a crack in the cylinder head or even the engine block. If you suspect an internal engine-coolant leak, keep a careful watch on the coolant level in your coolant-recovery tank or radiator. When there is a coolant leak, the level will drop as the coolant is dissipated out of the tailpipe. You will also notice the engine running hotter, and there might be tiny bubbles forming in the coolant-recovery tank while the engine is running. You can usually see these bubbles pop to the surface in the coolant-recovery tank. Check your owner's manual for the location of the coolant-recovery tank, or ask your mechanic to point it out.

Two: In extreme cases the coolant leaking into the cylinder might prevent that cylinder from firing. This results in a rough engine idle and reduced engine power. One of the best early warnings of an internal engine-coolant leak is the presence of antifreeze on the tip of a spark plug removed from a misfiring engine. There are several methods mechanics use to confirm a suspected internal coolant leak. One of the quickest is to use a special device that draws vapor from the top of the radiator and passes it through a blue test liquid. If the vapor causes the liquid to turn yellow, a diagnosis of an internal coolant leak is confirmed. Your mechanic will need to partially disassemble the engine to repair the leak.

Burning Odor

Symptoms

This odor insults the olfactory senses, as though you'd accidentally turned on the flame under a frying pan or pot handle. There isn't much smoke, but as the handle burns it gives off a strong odor that seems to clutch at your nose and cause a sort of gagging feeling. Unlike a burning plastic garment bag, this odor is heavy and almost reminds you of propane gas.

Explanation

This odor is the result of brake shoes overheating or a clutch slipping. See Diagnoses and Solutions for explanations of the causes of these two conditions.

Diagnoses and Solutions

One: Try to determine which end of the car the odor is coming from. If you suspect the odor is from the rear, you might have forgotten to release the parking brake. When you drive long enough with the parking brake engaged, the rear brake shoes begin to overheat and give off a strong burnt-plastic odor. If the brake was on briefly, there probably isn't any damage. If you left it on for a long trip, it would be wise to have the rear brake lining checked. In the meantime, simply disengage the parking brake and drive normally.

Two: If the odor is coming from the rear wheels and you did not find the parking brake engaged, there is a possibility that the rear brakes are not releasing. This can happen when a parking-brake cable becomes rusted and jams in its housing. Even though you have released the brake, the jammed cable holds the parking brake on. This causes the rear brakes to overheat and give off a burning odor. It might also cause the car to drag and not roll freely. In extreme cases the rear wheels will begin to smoke. If you suspect the parking brake is not disengaging, there is a simple test you can do to check. In an open, safe area, drive the car at about 30 miles per hour, then take your foot off the gas. The car should roll freely until you apply the brakes. If you find the car slows down quickly, the parking brake is applied. Another way to check is to jack up the rear of the car so that you can turn both rear wheels by hand. Put the transmission in neutral and try turning the wheels. If the wheels won't move, the parking brake is probably applied. The car may move again once the brakes cool, but not for long. You will need to have a mechanic find the cause of the brakes locking.

Three: If you believe the odor is coming from the front wheels, there is the possibility that the front brakes are overheating. Immediately after new brakes are installed, it is not unusual to detect a faint odor for a short time while the front brake pads break in. This odor should not last more than a hour. If a burning odor from new or old front brakes persists, the front brake calipers might be jamming in the partially on position. A front brake caliper is kind of like a vise that is powered by hydraulic pressure. If the pistons within the caliper become rusted, they can seize in the on position. This causes the brake pads to overheat as the car rolls. If only one caliper is seizing, the car will probably pull to one side when you brake. Whenever you have brake pads replaced, be sure the mechanic checks for binding or leaking brake calipers. The best time to rebuild or replace calipers is when the brake pads are being replaced. Worn or rusted brake hardware can also cause the brake calipers to drag and overheat the brake pads.

Four: If your car is equipped with a standard transmission, you might experience the burnt pot-handle odor when the clutch begins to slip. This will occur because of a worn or misadjusted clutch. The clutch disc should slip slightly as you engage the clutch, then lock with the pressure plate and flywheel. If this does not occur there is movement between the clutch disc, flywheel, and pressure plate, which causes wear and overheating of the clutch disc. This odor can occur when the car is driven by an inexperienced driver who does not know how to properly engage the clutch; or it might simply be that the clutch needs to be adjusted or replaced. Whichever is the cause, the odor of a burning clutch should not be ignored. Have the car inspected. The telltale proof that your clutch is slipping comes when engine rpms increase without the car going any faster. An adjustment may help, but you will probably need a new clutch sooner or later.

Smell of Burning Oil

Symptoms

After you have driven for a while and the engine has warmed up, you begin to smell a strong odor that reminds you of that time when you burnt the oil in a frying pan on the stove; or perhaps it might smell like your barbecue just after you have ignited the charcoal lighter fluid. You might seem to smell the odor coming from the heater or air conditioner. You might see wisps of smoke coming from under the hood.

Explanation

Normally, you shouldn't smell burning oil when your engine is running. If there is this odor, more than likely oil, transmission fluid, or power-steering fluid is leaking onto a hot surface. That surface could be the hot exhaust manifold, the sides of the engine cylinder heads, or the exhaust system.

Diagnoses and Solutions

One: The old adage "where there is smoke there is fire" might not hold entirely true, but don't dismiss the odor of burning oil as just something old cars do. The first place to check for the cause of a burning oil odor is under the hood. Look at the long, rectangular metal box known as the rocker-arm cover or covers. They are similar on most engines. If you see a shiny layer of oil at the point where the rocker-arm cover fastens to the cylinder head (the part of the engine to which the cover is attached), you have a rocker-arm-cover gasket leak. This allows engine oil to leak down over the hot exhaust manifold and actually bake. The odor you smell is baking oil. If that oil were to get hot enough, it could burst into flame. Oil leaking from the rocker-arm-cover gaskets will also drip onto the ignition wires and spark plugs on many engines. The area where the rocker-arm-cover gasket seals the rocker-arm cover to the cylinder head should be clean. If there is a leak here, have the rocker-arm-cover gasket replaced.

Two: Motor oil leaking from the intake-manifold gasket on many V8 and V6 engines will leak down either the front or the rear of the engine. This oil will also appear in the form of a shiny black area at the point where the intake-manifold gasket seals the intake manifold to the engine block. It is less common than a rocker-arm-cover gasket leak. You'll still need to have a mechanic replace the intake-manifold gasket.

Three: Any oil leak that allows oil to drip onto the exhaust pipes, muffler, or catalytic cover will cause a burning oil odor. As part of your check for the source of a burning oil odor, be sure to look under the car for evidence of oil leaking onto any part of the exhaust system. Remember that the oil cannot come from the exhaust system; it drips onto the hot exhaust and burns. A mechanic will have to determine the source of the oil. It may be from the engine, transmission, or power-steering system.

Four: The fluid from your automatic transmission can also leak out of the back of the transmission or at the side. This type of leak might allow transmission fluid to hit the hot exhaust pipe and create a burning odor. A transmission seal may be needed—a job you'll need to have a mechanic take care of.

Five: Another source of burning oil is a leak from the power-steering system. Drips that hit a hot surface will give off a burning odor. Have a mechanic diagnose and repair any leaks from the power-steering pump, power-steering gear, or rack-and-pinion steering assembly; or it might come from a leaking power-steering hose. This is the most dangerous.

CAUTION: A leaking power-steering pressure hose can spray hot fluid on a hot surface such as the exhaust manifold, causing the power-steering fluid to burst into flame. If you suspect the power-steering has been leaking fluid, don't waste any time. Take the car to a mechanic as soon as possible.

Smell of Burning Plastic

Symptoms

The odor of burning plastic is quite different from the odor of burning oil. It is more irritating to your nose and eyes. It might remind you of the time you left a plastic spoon too close to a flame, or it might smell like the toaster the day it shorted out. There are several types of plastics now used in cars, so it is not always possible to know precisely what is burning when you smell burnt plastic.

Explanation

Any unusual odor should tip you off to an impending problem. A burning odor of any type is caused by something. In the case of a plastic bag, it is nothing serious; but in the case of battery cable burning against a hot manifold, it can be serious. This odor is also caused by a parking brake left on while driving, brake pads burning, and electrical shorts. See Diagnoses and Solutions for explanations of these possible causes. Determine the cause of the odor as soon as possible.

Diagnoses and Solutions

One: By far the most common source of burning plastic in a passenger car is caused by a plastic bag sticking to the exhaust system. The first thing you should do when you smell the odor of burning plastic in your car is to get out and look under the car for evidence of a plastic bag.

Two: If there is nothing stuck to the exhaust that is causing the odor, sniff around each of the wheels. A parking brake left on or brakes that are not working correctly will cause the brake pads or linings to burn. (See also pages 127–129.)

Three: Electrical shorts can also cause a burning odor, as the plastic covering over electrical wires overheats. Most of a car's wiring is protected by fuses, and generally the fuse will blow long before a wire melts. However, there are certain wires that are not protected by fuses. The heavy battery cables from the battery to the starter are not fused. If one of these wires is shorted it can burn and cause a burning odor. Electric motors like the starter, blower, and power windows can give off a burning plastic odor when they become shorted. If you suspect an electrical problem, the best way to prevent further damage is to disconnect the battery until a mechanic can diagnose the problem. However, be careful when opening the hood, to make sure there is not a raging fire under the hood that will flare up.

CAUTION: If smoke is billowing from under the hood, don't open it. Call the fire department. Whatever you do, don't touch any electrical wiring. It might be very hot without appearing to be shorted.

Gasoline Odor

Symptoms

The odor might be present right after you fill up with gasoline, or it might come after the car warms up. In some cases you might smell it only when you open the trunk or at one part of the car or another. Wherever you notice the odor of gasoline, it is a warning signal.

Explanation

Gasoline odors come from leaks in fuel-injection lines, fuel tanks, vapor controls, fuel pumps, or elsewhere in the fuel system. See Diagnoses and Solutions for explanations of the possible sources.

Diagnoses and Solutions

One: As soon as you become aware of the odor of gasoline in or around your car, it is time to take action. Gasoline is the most dangerous liquid you carry onboard any car or truck. If you're on the highway, pull off as soon as you can find a safe place that will put you well out of the way of oncoming traffic. Shut off the engine and pull the hood release. Open the hood. Be sure you're not smoking a cigarette, pipe, or cigar. Look over the engine for signs of liquid. If there was a strong gasoline odor when you opened the hood, don't attempt to restart the engine unless you are absolutely sure there are no leaks. Pay particular attention to the area around the carburetor and fuel filter on older cars. On newer fuel-injected cars, look for wet gasoline on top of the engine near the spark plugs and the fuel-injector hoses or lines. Many fuel-injected cars have a very high fuel pressure. When a leak develops, it can send fuel spraying out of a defective line.

> **CAUTION: Gasoline leaks at the top of the engine are the most dangerous because the gasoline can be ignited by the engine's own ignition system or by heat from the exhaust manifolds. If there is any sign of a gasoline leak on top of the engine, do not restart the engine. Call for a tow truck.**

Two: Assuming you have carefully checked the top of the engine for leaks and there are none, go to the rear of the car and look underneath in the area of the fuel tank. Check for any signs of leaks along the bottom surface of the tank. If there is a leak, it might dribble down the sides of the tank. If the gasoline tank is covered with an undercoating, a gasoline leak will soften the coating, making it glisten and possibly wash away. Eventually there will be a drip of gasoline on the floor under the gasoline tank. In an emergency, fuel-tank leaks can be repaired using a special epoxy made for that purpose. In an emergency, cut a piece of wood to block up the hole. Check the local auto-supply store for a temporary fuel-tank repair kit, which comes with instructions. Eventually the fuel tank will have to be removed and repaired, using solder and possibly a section of sheet metal. If there is a major leak or tear in the tank, it might have to be replaced. Anytime there is a gasoline leak it may be dangerous to start the engine. If there are puddles of gasoline it would be safer to call for a tow truck.

Three: Most cars with fuel injection have the fuel pump inside the fuel tank. However, some have the fuel pump bolted to the chassis at the rear of the car between the fuel pump and the engine. Generally you will find this type of external electric fuel pump toward the rear of the car. With the key turned on but the engine not running, look for signs of fuel leaking from the fuel pump or lines.

Older cars with carburetors generally have a mechanical fuel pump mounted on the engine. Mechanical fuel pumps rarely leak unless the engine is running. To find a leak on this type of pump, you must run the engine. First visually check the mechanical fuel pump. If it appears to be freshly washed, it might have a fuel leak. To check for sure, have someone start the engine while you observe the pump. Do not use a 110-volt trouble lamp; use a flashlight only. If there is a leak and gasoline were to splash on a hot trouble lamp, the bulb could explode. While you are checking the pump, take a good look at the short rubber hoses that connect the fuel pump to the metal fuel lines. This rubber hose can loosen, crack, or break and cause a fuel leak. Whenever you smell gasoline there is probably a leak somewhere. If the odor is strong, it would be wiser not to attempt to start until it can be checked by a mechanic.

Four: Metal fuel lines on older cars can rust to the point where they leak gasoline. If no leaks are found in the tank, fuel pump, or on top of the engine, have a mechanic put the car on a lift and carefully check every inch of the metal fuel lines. Often the leak will occur in a tight spot where the fuel lines are fastened to the chassis. The mechanic should look for accumulated rust on fuel and brake lines.

Mildew Odor

Symptoms

Mildew has an unmistakable odor. You have probably smelled it in a damp basement or in a boat. It wrinkles the nose and torments the nostrils. In a car it can be penetrating to the point where it actually soaks into your clothes when you drive in the car. Even after you have left the car, the odor seems to linger all around you.

CAUTION: Gasoline is a miracle source of power for cars, but it is taken for granted and treated like a friend. It only takes a cupful of gasoline to duplicate the explosive force of a stick of dynamite. Treat any gasoline odor as a top priority. Gasoline leaking over the top of an engine can suddenly burst into flames and destroy the car before the fire department can respond. Gasoline can be spread by a broken fuel-injection line or hose. In this case the fire can be very intense. Gasoline leaking under the car is not quite as dangerous, but is still a major threat. Under most modern cars there is a catalytic converter, which becomes very hot when driving. Gasoline sprayed on a hot catalytic converter is highly flammable. When you smell gasoline, take it seriously and seek help in finding out the cause.

If you have a lawn mower, outboard motor, or power saw, you might be in the habit of carrying a can of gasoline around in the trunk. Some car owners do so to keep from being stranded without gasoline on a lonely road. Never carry gasoline in your car trunk and never consider carrying a gasoline can in the car. In a collision, a five-gallon can of gasoline in the trunk or, worse yet, in the passenger compartment, can rupture and spray gasoline over the trunk or passenger compartment. That can of gasoline can turn a collision into a catastrophe. Treat gasoline like the high-explosive liquid it is. Don't smoke around it. Don't use it on your charcoal fire. Don't store it in your garage or basement, and don't use it as a cleaning solution. DON'T EVER CARRY GASOLINE IN A CONTAINER IN YOUR CAR.

Explanation

The odor of mildew in an automobile comes from water soaking into the carpets, seat upholstery, or insulation. Whenever you detect the odor of mildew in your car, it is wise to determine the cause as soon as possible. If water from the air-conditioner drain, for example, is allowed to continually leak into the car, it will damage the carpet and rust the metal flooring. A leaking trunk seal will allow water to damage items in the trunk and cause rust. Early detection will save you costly repairs. Left uncorrected, rust can develop in the trunk, in the doors, and on the floor. Rust weakens the metal and will cause its eventual destruction (see page 261).

Diagnoses and Solutions

One: If mildew is caused by a small isolated spill of water from a container or from having left a window open, it will probably dry up and go away of its own accord, provided you leave the windows open in good weather to air out the car. Once the water-soaked area has dried out, your troubles should be over.

Two: Where there is no apparent spill of water, the problem of mildew is more serious. Most often it is caused by a clogged air-conditioner drain. All car air conditioners remove water from the air that is blown across the cooling device of the air-conditioner evaporator. If that water leaks into the car it will soak the rugs and insulation. You can generally find evidence of mildew and water-soaking on the upper part of the front passenger-side floor. If you find the carpet wet in that area, check for a clogged air-conditioner drain. Most cars have an air-conditioner water drain on the passenger side, under the hood, at the base of the bulkhead on the bottom of the air-conditioner housing. If you attempt to clear the drain, be sure to use a wooden or plastic stick. Never push a metal object into the air-conditioner drain. Doing so could puncture the air-conditioner evaporator and cause costly damage to the air conditioner. Note that the color and texture of the water is very important. If the water is clear, it is either drain or rain water. If it is greenish or yellowish and oily to the touch, it might be caused by a leaking heater core. A leaking heater core will allow engine coolant to leak into the car at the passenger-side floor. It might also cause window fogging. This will need repair by a mechanic.

Three: Water can also leak into the car from the air vents located just below the windshields on many cars. The vents are designed to allow air into the car and prevent water from entering. The water is drained off through tubes or rubber valves. If the drains become clogged with leaves or dirt, the vent areas will back up with water and the water will spill into the passenger compartment. If you find the right pas-senger-side floor wet after a heavy rainstorm, check for clogged vent drains. This can be done by using a garden hose to run water into the vent from outside the car. The water should run easily out of the vent drains. If not, see your mechanic.

Four: Water can also leak into the car from gaskets on the door. Door drains may clog. You can check for clogged door drains by looking at the base of the car door with the doors open. You will find areas where the metal has a hole or slot designed to allow any water that gets down past the glass to drain out. One good tipoff to water in the door is the sound of sloshing water coming from the door when you brake or accelerate.

Five: Water leaking into the trunk can also cause mildew. Very often it goes undetected because you seldom use the trunk. When you do open the trunk, the mildew odor hits you squarely in the nose. In addition, mildew can damage items left in the trunk. Water leaks into the trunk are often difficult to locate and even more difficult to stop. Take the car to a mechanic or to a body shop for repair.

Steamy, Slightly Sweet-Smelling Odor

Symptoms

It is raining, or the weather has turned cold and the windshield has fogged up. You switch on the defroster, and instead of the windshield clearing, it seems to get worse. There might also be the odor of steam, which reminds you of the heavy, humid feeling you get when you walk into a heated pool down at the Y or your favorite health club. The difference is that the chlorine odor will be replaced by a too-sweet odor you feel in your nostrils.

Explanation

Engine coolant is used to heat your car. Hot coolant from the engine is piped through the wall between the passenger compartment and the engine compartment. The hot coolant is passed through a sort of miniradiator, where the air from the passenger compartment is blown through and heated. Everything works fine until the little radiator or heater core develops a leak. If it is a major leak, the floor on the passenger side will fill with greenish or yellowish engine coolant and steam vapor will pour out of the defroster ducts. If it is a small leak the evidence will be window fogging, a steamy, sweet odor, and possibly a few drops of coolant at the air-conditioner-drain hose.

Diagnoses and Solutions

One: A sweet, steamy odor from the defroster ducts is usually a sign of a leak in the heater core. What is happening is that coolant from the engine is seeping through a tiny hole in the heater core and being blown out of the defroster ducts onto the windshield. The sweet odor comes from the anti-freeze mixed with water to form the coolant used in your engine's cooling system. One sure way to detect a leaking heater core is to check the air-conditioner drain hose for drops of green or yellowish coolant. You will generally find the drain hose under the hood, to the right side, at the base of the air conditioner. The telltale evidence of coolant drops at the base of the heater core or on the right-side passenger floor, inside the car, is proof positive that you are in for the expense of having the heater core repaired or replaced. Heater cores are usually costly to replace because they are located inside the dash on the right and require extensive disassembly to replace.

Two: The same sweet-smelling steam odor occurs when there is a coolant leak around the top of the engine. If coolant accumulates on the intake manifold or in any pockets around the top of a hot engine, it will eventually heat up and the odor will be drawn into the heater or air-conditioner vents. When you smell a steamy, sweet odor, look for signs of a leaking heater core and also check for a coolant leak around the engine and radiator. The heater is most often located in the dash behind the glove compartment.

CAUTION: Evidence of a heater leak should not be ignored. The coolant that is leaking is being drained from your engine. If the engine-coolant level reaches a low enough point, the engine will overheat. Because the engine coolant operates under pressure, the heater leak will get worse as the engine-coolant pressure rises. What might start out as a poorly operating windshield de-fogger can, before you reach home, become a billowing steam vapor that forces you to leave the car.

Miscellaneous Malfunctions

Battery Goes Dead

Symptoms

You get into the car, buckle up your seat belt, and switch the ignition key to the start position. Instead of the normal *varoom* sound you expect to hear, there is either no sound at all or a dull clicking sound. Your temper rises as you realize your battery is dead.

Explanation

Batteries go dead because they have been discharged of power or are simply worn out. See Diagnoses and Solutions for possible causes.

Diagnoses and Solutions

One: When your battery is dead there is nothing that will start the car except a booster battery or a recharge of your battery, assuming it will take a charge. The first order of business, then, is getting the engine started so that you can find out what happened. Before you attempt to boost a dead battery, carefully read the section How to Safely Boost a Dead Battery, page 194. There is a wrong way and a right way you should know about, even if you have boosted your car a dozen times and think you know exactly how it should be done. You next need to know why the battery went dead to make sure it doesn't happen again. (See solutions Two through Five.)

Two: Check to see if you left the headlights on or perhaps twisted the headlight switch so that the dome lights stayed on overnight. This can happen on many cars. Curiously, a battery that can turn a powerful starter motor and run all of the lights on your car for half an hour without a problem can also be fully discharged by a dome-light bulb left on overnight. Make sure you didn't leave the lights on.

Three: Often a battery becomes discharged because the glove compartment or trunk light did not go out when you closed the glove box or trunk lid. Because it is difficult to tell if those lights went out, you can either remove the fuses or bulbs as a test to see if the battery remains charged, or you can have a mechanic check for electrical drains.

Four: One other common cause for the battery going dead is a loose alternator belt. You can check for a loose belt on most cars by trying to turn the alternator fan with your thumb and fingers. You'll find the alternator fan on the front of the alternator, just behind the fan belt. Make sure you don't try this with the engine running. If you can turn the little fan, the belt is probably too loose. Belt-tension check gauges are also available at auto-supply stores.

Five: If none of the previous solutions helps, you need the services of a mechanic who can do a complete charging-system checkup on your car. Don't assume the battery is bad simply because it went dead. Batteries do go dead and do wear out on their own, but far too often car owners replace a perfectly good battery before they have diagnosed the cause of the problem.

> **CAUTION:** Batteries can be dangerous and can explode in your face; read page 194 before you work around a battery. Keep your fingers clear of the belts when the engine is running, and be aware that the alternator fan can do serious damage if you get hit by one of the blades. On cars with separate electric radiator-cooling fans, the fan can come on when the engine is warm, even if you have the ignition turned off.

Windshield Wipers Don't Work

Symptoms

The wipers leave streaks across the glass, which distort your vision and are particularly annoying when driving at night.

Explanation

The most frequent problem drivers have with wipers is that they move across the windshield but don't really clean the glass. The problem is either worn wiper blades, a bent wiper arm, a blown wiper fuse, or a clogged or malfunctioning wiper-tank pump. See Diagnoses and Solutions for explanations of these conditions.

Diagnoses and Solutions

One: Wiper blades do wear out so, if yours have been on the car for years, don't even think about it. Replace the wiper blades, but clean the windshield carefully before you install the new wiper blades. Acid rain and all the awful stuff that we pump into the air eventually comes back down with the rain. The accumulation on your windshield could contain all sorts of nasty dirt such as soot, sand, salt, oil, minerals, bits of rubber, asbestos, and more. Cleaning your windshield on a regular basis is the best way to keep the wipers working well. Remember to carefully clean the area where the wipers park and to wipe off the wiper blades. Use a good-quality windshield-washer solvent that will help clean the glass. In very dirty and dusty areas, you might try adding one teaspoon of liquid dishwasher detergent to the windshield-washer jar for each quart of water. Don't use the type of detergent that makes bubbles.

CAUTION: If you try replacing your own wiper blades, make sure you have fully engaged the little tangs that hold the wiper to the refill. If you miss one of the tangs, the wiper might eventually scratch the windshield.

Two: If your problem is that the wipers don't work at all, check the fuse panel first. The location of fuse panels varies widely between makes. Check the owner's manual for the location. A blown fuse will disable the wipers and usually indicates a problem in the wiper electrical circuit. There is one trick you can try if you find that the wiper fuse is not burnt out. Gently grasp the wiper arm and carefully wriggle it up and down. Sometimes the linkage jams, and a gentle tug might free it.

Three: Windshield-washer tanks sometimes pick up dirt. If you find the windshield washer won't spray washer solvent on the glass, check for a clogged filter on the hose that can be found under the cap of a great many windshield-washer tanks. The washer tank is generally under the hood and made of white plastic. See the owner's manual. Be sure to keep washer solvent in the tank. If you live in an area where temperatures go below freezing, use a solvent that will not freeze. When the solvent freezes, the windshield washer won't work, and damage to the washer pump can result.

Heater or Defroster Doesn't Work

Symptoms

You roll out of bed on a dark winter morning and fight the winter chill until you're safe inside your car. Then you start up and wait for the heater to start delivering warm air. When the heater is working normally, it still seems to take forever for the air blowing out on your feet to become warm. On this day, the air seems to actually get colder or perhaps just a little warm. As you drive with your fingers stinging from the pain of the ice-cold steering wheel, you wonder what could be wrong with the heater.

Explanation

For a heater or defroster to work properly, several things have to happen. First and foremost is that the coolant must reach a sufficient temperature to heat the heater core. Once that occurs, the blower fan must force passenger-compartment air over the heated coils of the heater core. For this to happen, the heater blower motor has to work. In addition, the doors that direct the heated air to the heater ducts must be correctly positioned. If there is a malfunction in the heater control that does not cause the doors to switch from air conditioning to heating, the heater core might be getting hot, but you will not be getting hot air in the car. The same might be true if you find the heated air blows to your feet but will not blow out of the defroster ducts. On very new cars, the heater/air conditioner might be controlled by a computer. In this case there is no choice but to enlist the services of a mechanic skilled in the diagnosis of computer-controlled heater/air-conditioner systems.

Diagnoses and Solutions

One: Check the temperature control lever to be sure it is moved to the hot position. As you move the lever on most cars, you will feel some resistance as the lever pulls on a wire cable. If the lever suddenly seems to move easier than normally, there is a good probability that the inside part of the lever or cable is broken. On push-button or automatic systems the diagnosis is more complicated; read on. See your mechanic for this repair.

Two: Check the coolant level in the radiator. Make sure the engine coolant is not hot and under pressure. Do not attempt to remove the radiator cap unless you can comfortably grasp the upper radiator hose without burning your fingers. Feel the hose to be sure there is no pressure in the cooling system. If the hose is difficult to squeeze, the system is still under pressure. If it can be easily collapsed and is cool to the touch, it is safe to remove the radiator cap. A low coolant level will prevent the heated coolant from flowing through the heater core. When this happens, the heater and defroster cannot blow heated air. Fill the radiator (see page 258) and coolant-recovery tank (see page 81). After the engine has again cooled down to where you can safely remove the radiator cap, recheck the coolant level. If you find the radiator or coolant-recovery tank low on coolant, have your mechanic check the cooling system for coolant leaks. Read Understanding Your Car's Cooling System, page 258.

Three: If the coolant level in the radiator is up to the top and the fan still blows cold air for a very long time but eventually the air is heated, check for an engine thermostat that is not closing. The thermostat is a little valve in the cooling system that keeps the engine coolant from flowing through the radiator until it is warm enough. If the thermostat remains open, it takes a very long time for the heater or defroster to blow warm air. Replacing a thermostat is a simple job on most cars, but it's probably wiser for you to have it done by a mechanic. One common mistake backyard mechanics make when replacing a thermostat is to install the new thermostat upside down. Another is to improperly seat the thermostat, causing the water-outlet housing to crack. You can buy a simplified repair manual, designed for do-it-yourselfers, for most cars. These manuals are sold at book stores and larger auto-supply stores.

Four: If the coolant is hot, it might not be flowing through the heater core, either because the heater control valve is not opening or the heater core is clogged. The heater control valve is generally located near the back of the engine. You can trace the garden-hose-size heater hoses from the fire-wall—that is, the wall between the engine and the passenger compartment—or heater/air-conditioner housing to the engine. The valve is generally between the engine and one of the hoses going to the heater core. The other hose coming from the fire wall or heater/air-conditioner housing will have no valve. Once you know which hoses are the heater hoses, you can try a little test mechanics use to find out if the hot coolant is flowing through the heater core.

CAUTION: This test has to be done with the engine running and you could, if careless, get a finger or your long hair caught up in a belt or even the engine fan. Do not attempt this test if you are not fully aware of the risks of touching a running engine.

The idea of this test is to feel the heat on both heater hoses. When the heater system is working, both hoses should feel hot to the touch, right up to the heater valve and heater core. The outlet hose from the heater should also be hot. If the hose is hot up to the heater valve and the hoses after the heater valve and the return hose to the engine are cool, the heater valve is probably not opening. The heater cannot get hot if the valve stays closed. This could be caused by a broken cable, if it is a cable-controlled valve, or by a loss of vacuum if the valve is vacuum-controlled. One simple way to test, if you suspect that your trouble is a valve that doesn't open, is to remove both hoses from the valve and install a short pipe nipple in place of the heater valve. If the heater then gets hot, have the valve replaced.

Five: All of the foregoing solutions are based on the assumption that the heater blower is working. If your problem is that the warm air only comes in when you drive along and there is no warm air blowing in when you switch on the blower, first check the fuse box for a blown fuse (see the owner's manual for fuse box location). If the heater/air-conditioner fuses are good, listen for the sound of the blower motor, generally located on the right front side of the car, either under the dash or under the hood. If you cannot hear the blower motor, try moving the control switch and the control lever to various positions. If the blower works in some positions but not in others, the problem is in the control. If you cannot hear the blower working in any position, check for disconnected wires on the blower motor. Blower motors must have a power supply and must also be grounded to the battery negative through the car body. If the ground is poor, the blower motor will not work. If the power supply is disconnected, the blower will not work. Here again you will probably need the help of an auto electrician. Most heater/air-conditioner systems use a resistor block to create several blower speeds. A disconnected or defective resistor block can act like a defective blower motor. Before condemning the blower motor, test it with a direct jumper wire to battery voltage. If you want to try this repair yourself, first buy a copy of the do-it-yourself type of repair manual for your specific make and model.

CAUTION: Whenever you work around the engine there is the risk of being burnt by hot coolant or being struck by the engine fan. In addition, there is the risk of being caught up in a fan belt, which can chop off a finger or catch long hair. There is also the risk of being shocked by the high-voltage electrical current in the ignition system. Before you poke around a running engine, it is wise to be sure you understand all of the risks of personal injury.

Air Conditioner Doesn't Work

Symptoms

The weather turns suddenly hot. You switch on the air-conditioner control lever to cold and turn up the blower-fan switch. Instead of the cold breeze you expected, you feel a blast of hot air coming from the air-conditioner vents.

Explanation

There are many reasons why an air conditioner will not blow cold air. For the air conditioner to work, a full cycle of refrigerant compressing, cooling, and expanding must occur; see page 262, About Air Conditioners. In years gone by, car owners simply added a little refrigerant gas to the system when they thought it wasn't cooling well. Older systems had a sight glass that revealed bubbles when refrigerant gas was needed. Sight glasses are no longer used on car air conditioners, and the price of refrigerant has skyrocketed. What used to cost $1.50 a pound is now approaching $10.00 a pound. It has also been determined that refrigerant gas damages the ozone layer of our atmosphere. The point is that when a leak occurs in your air conditioner, don't simply add gas. Have a competent mechanic find out why the gas was lost. Electronic leak detectors are in use by up-to-date mechanics to pinpoint the source of a leak. Refrigerant gas is too costly to waste. Ask your mechanic if he has the equipment to recycle the gas you have when doing repairs. Not all repairs require a full charge of refrigerant gas. It can and should be saved and reused. Charging the system yourself can put you at physical risk and you might be overcharging the system, which can result in costly damage.

Diagnoses and Solutions

One: The most common problem here is a loss of refrigerant gas. Refrigerant gas is also known by the brand name Freon or R-12. R-12 has been found to damage the environment and is soon to be replaced by a gas or gases that are kinder to our atmosphere. In the meantime, if your car was built to run on R-12 you must have a sufficient supply of the stuff for the air conditioner to work; it will not work on safer gases. One quick way to check for a loss of R-12 is to check the air-conditioner compressor clutch. You will find the clutch at the front of the air-conditioner compressor. The clutch connects the air-conditioner belt to the compressor. When the compressor is turned on, the clutch must engage for the belt to drive the compressor. If the electrical connections are okay, the clutch should engage a strong magnet, causing the metal center of the clutch to begin spinning with the pulley. When the air conditioner is off, that center plate, about four or five inches in diameter, does not spin. If turning on the air conditioner does not engage the clutch, chances are the system is out of refrigerant gas and has been shut off by the low-pressure switch. Ask your mechanic to check for a loss of refrigerant. If there is a loss, make sure a leak test is done to determine the reason. Most mechanics use an electronic leak detector.

Two: Where the air-conditioner clutch cycles on and off rapidly, the system might also be low on refrigerant.

Three: On many imported and some domestic cars there is a separate clutch shut-off switch. Before you go for a refrigerant recharge, make sure the air-conditioner clutch switch is engaged. If it is, use a test lamp at the clutch wiring-harness itself to see if 12-volt current is arriving to power the clutch. If the test lamp lights you probably have a defective clutch. If there is no current, the problem might be in the wiring circuit, a fuse, or an air-conditioner control switch.

CAUTION: Refrigerant gas can be dangerous. Always wear eye protection when you are handling refrigerant gas or doing any work around your car air-conditioner system. If a fitting breaks or a hose bursts, the surge of refrigerant gas can freeze and burn your skin. If it squirts into your eyes it could cause serious damage. Avoid inhaling refrigerant gas and never work on your air conditioner without proper ventilation. If refrigerant gas is drawn into the engine and burned in the combustion chamber, it can produce toxic gases at the tailpipe. Anything more than changing a fuse on your car air conditioner will probably require the services of a competent mechanic trained in the proper handling of refrigerant gas. It would be wise to obtain either the complete repair-shop manual or a condensed version before you attempt any wiring checks or other similar tests.

Dash Lights Don't Work

Symptoms

You notice it the moment you turn on the headlights and can't see the speedometer or other gauges on the instrument panel; or it might be that the light is very dim.

Diagnoses and Solutions

One: If the fuse is good, there might be a problem with the rheostat that controls the brightness of the dash lights. On some cars you simply twist the headlight switch to adjust the brightness of the dash lights. Try turning the switch all the way in either direction. Be careful: On some cars, turning the headlight switch all the way in one direction will put on the dome lights. If you forget the switch in the on position, it will keep the dome lights on and discharge the battery. If turning the headlight or a separate headlight-dimmer control switch does not help, the problem might be the headlight switch itself. Headlight switches are tricky to replace and require special tools. Check with the service manual before you attempt to replace a headlight switch.

Two: If there are no dash lights at all, check for a blown instrument-panel light fuse. Fuses are generally located in the fuse panel under the dash (see your owner's manual for the exact location on your car). On many cars the circuits are designed so that the fuse for the instrument-panel lights will blow out when the taillights or other lights aren't working. If you find a blown fuse, replace it with a new fuse, and make sure you check all the other lights as well.

Three: If only part of the instrument panel is not illuminated, some of the dash lamp bulbs might be out. Here again, it is tricky on most cars to replace dash bulbs. Do not attempt it without first checking the correct procedure in the repair manual.

Four: On cars with modern digital instrument panels, where the speed is shown in numbers rather than on a meter dial, it is generally difficult to repair this system. Often the entire instrument panel or sections of it are replaced as a unit. This will require professional help.

CAUTION: Before attempting any repairs under the dash or to any part of the electrical system, disconnect the battery. It is very easy to touch the wrong wire and cause a short that will burn the wiring. Be careful about attaching wires unless you know precisely what you are connecting and to what you are connecting it. Even with the battery disconnected, you can create a short that will burn wires once you connect the battery. Never put a wire or wrap foil on a fuse. Fuses are designed to protect the wiring; bypassing a fuse can cause costly damage to the car's wiring. Remember, disconnect the battery first before you do any wiring under the dash or under the hood.

Headlights Don't Work

Symptoms

Your first indication may be flashing headlights from another driver trying to warn you that your headlights are out. Or while driving at night, you may see the road ahead brighter on one side than another. You may find that when you switch from high beams to low beams, or vice versa, the road gets darker on one side. Either way, the warning means to check your headlights to see if all the beams are working. Check all the lamps on both high-beam and low-beam settings. If one or more headlights are not lighted when they should be, start by checking the lamps first.

Explanation

Headlamps come in various shapes and sizes. Older cars use a single headlamp, which might work normally on low but have a burnt-out element for the high beams. With this type of light, you might find one headlight goes out when you switch the dimmer switch but comes back on when you again switch the dimmer. On more complicated systems, there are two headlamps that have double elements—one for high beam and one for low beam—like the old headlamps. However, they also have a separate inner headlamp that only goes on when the high-beam (country) lamps are used.

Diagnoses and Solutions

One: Check out the way your headlamps should work before you have a problem. Have a friend switch on the headlights and work the dimmer switch while you watch the lights.

In this way you will have a better idea what is wrong when there is a problem. Make checking your headlights and cleaning them of dirt and grime a part of your monthly maintenance check.

Two: If one headlamp is out in the low-beam position but comes on when you switch the headlight-dimmer switch, most likely the problem is a headlamp bulb with one burnt-out element. Try installing a new headlamp bulb, but make sure the new headlamp bulb has exactly the same number as the old one.

Three: If both headlamp bulbs are out all of the time in both high-beam and low-beam dimmer-switch positions, more than likely your problem is a blown fuse or burnt-out headlight switch. Check the fuses first, then the connections to the headlight switch. Before having the headlight switch replaced, be sure the wiring to the headlamp-dimmer switch is connected and the switch is working properly.

Four: Older cars generally have a foot-operated headlamp-dimmer switch. It is possible for this switch to go bad, so that both headlamps are out in either the high-beam or low-beam position. It is also possible for the wires to become disconnected from this switch and prevent either headlamp from working in the high or low position. New cars have the headlamp-dimmer switch mounted on the steering column. This switch works essentially the same as the old floor-mounted type. If it becomes defective, the headlamps might also go out when the dimmer switch is operated. Have your mechanic check and replace the switch if necessary.

> **CAUTION:** Always check for burnt-out fuses before changing any lamps or switches. Although it is unlikely that both headlamp bulbs could be burnt out at the same time, it is not impossible. Check the lamps before you replace switches. Always use a lamp with exactly the same number. When replacing headlamp bulbs, remove only the headlamp-retaining ring. Do not disturb the headlamp focus-adjusting screws. There are several different types of headlamps, so make sure the replacement lamp has the same part number. If your old headlamp was marked "halogen" be sure to install a new one marked the same.

Turn-Signal or Brake Lights Don't Work

Symptoms

Generally you discover your brake or signal lights aren't working when an irate motorist drives up alongside and loudly questions your intelligence for turning without signaling.

Explanation

The brake lights on most cars share the same lamps as the turn signals and the four-way emergency flashers; on many imports and newer cars there is a separate yellow turn-signal lamp. On recent vintage cars there is also a single brake light mounted on the shelf between the top of the rear seat and the rear windshield. These single brake lights are often called "cyclops" brake lights. All of these lamps are protected by fuses, so the fuse is the first thing to check (look in your owner's manual for the location of the fuse box). But when you check the system you should be aware that the circuits are generally routed through the turn signal switch on the steering column. This makes diagnosing the problem more complicated. Beyond replacing burned-out lamps, you will probably need the help of an auto electrician.

Diagnoses and Solutions

One: Your best insurance against being caught with your brake lights or turn signals not working is to check them once a month. A good time would be when you check the air in the tires. Develop a routine where you check all of your lights and the fluid levels in the engine, transmission, and cooling system. You'll need a friend to step on the brake when you check to be sure the brake lights are working.

Two: To check the lights on most cars, make sure the turn-signal switch is in the off or center position. On cars that use the same red lamp for rear turn signals and brake lights, leaving the turn-signal switch in a left or right turn will confuse the diagnosis. Have a friend step on the brake pedal and check to see if both sides light up. On cars with a center brake light, mounted generally on the shelf behind the rear seat at the rear window, that light should also go on when your friend steps on the brake. If all of the lights are out, check for a blown fuse (see your owner's manual for the fuse location). If the fuse is good, ask your mechanic to check the brake-light switch. On cars where red brake and turn signals share the same bulb, you can check the bulb easily by simply operating the turn signal. If the same light is out for the brake and the turn signal, your problem is likely a burnt-out bulb.

If the signal lights work on both sides but do not go on when you step on the brake, the problem is more than likely a brake-light switch. There is one further test. Where the four-way emergency flasher flashes the same red lights as are used for brake and turn signals, if the lamps work for the four-way flashers and the turn signals but not for the brake lights, you can be sure the problem is a brake-light switch. If both brake lights stay on all of the time, check for a shorted or misadjusted brake-light switch generally located just above the brake pedal. If both front signal lights and both rear brake/signal lights stay on, check to see if the four-way flasher switch is on. Then check the four-way flasher unit (see the owner's manual or a repair shop manual for its location).

Three: On a car where the brake and turn lights are one in the same, if you find that the brake lights and four-way emergency flashers work but the turn signals do not, your problem is more than likely the turn-signal flasher. The turn-signal flasher is really a little timer, like the little flashing bulb on Christmas tree lights. When it burns out, the lights do not flash or do not go on at all. The lights might also not flash and just stay on when one or more bulbs on the same side in the front or rear are burnt out. Visually check all the lamps in each lamp assembly.

Four: Some imported cars and new domestic cars are using a separate system where the turn signals are amber lamps in the rear and the brake and taillights are separate red lamps. These are actually easier to diagnose. When one of the amber lamps is out, the problem is probably a burnt-out bulb. When one of the red lamps is out, the problem is probably a burnt-out bulb. When both amber lamps are out, check for a bad turn-signal flasher. Check the owner's manual or a repair shop manual. When both red lamps are out, check for a bad brake-light switch. Although it is unlikely, it is also possible for both bulbs to burn out. Before assuming the trouble is a switch or flasher, remove and check the bulbs. You can usually see a broken filament wire in a defective lamp. Often the defective lamp turns black or cream-colored.

Five: Four-way emergency flashers use a separate flasher to control the flashing of the front turn-signal lamps and rear brake or signals lamps. When the rear lamps work for the stops or turn signals but not for the four-way emergency flashers, check for a burnt-out flasher first. The four-way flasher might be located right next to the turn-signal flasher, hidden up in the dash, or even placed on the passenger side of some cars. Most auto-supply stores have a flasher location chart that will help. Also see the owner's manual or a repair shop manual.

CAUTION: If you attempt to replace a turn-signal or brake-lamp bulb, be very careful to look at the base of the bulb. Most cars use a turn-signal lamp that is really two lamps in one. These have two small silver-colored protrusions at the base of the lamp. Some other cars use a lamp with just one protrusion. If you mistakenly install the wrong-type bulb, you might blow the fuse or, worse, create bizarre symptoms such as the dash lamps going on when you step on the brake pedal. Check the lamp numbers and make sure you use exactly the same lamp.

Transmission Stays in Low Gear (Automatic)

Symptoms

You accelerate away from a stop and find the transmission does not change to the next higher gear. The engine speed increases but the car seems to be dragging. There is plenty of power but the car won't really move along easily and the engine seems louder than normal.

Explanation

It takes more power at the wheels to get a car rolling from a dead stop. On a car with standard transmission you would manually shift into first gear, then when the car got rolling you would manually shift into second, then third as the car increases in speed, and so on. With an automatic transmission this shifting from first to second to third is accomplished by means of a series of valves and switches that control hydraulic pressure. When there is a failure in this controlling system the transmission stays in first or low gear. You hear the engine roaring loudly because the car is moving faster than it should in first gear. Also read page 244.

Diagnoses and Solutions

One: When the transmission selector is placed in the drive position, there should be a normal shift from first to second gear at about sixteen miles per hour. This would be the equivalent of your shifting a standard transmission from first to second gear. If this does not occur, the engine increases speed but the car does not gain speed normally. When this happens to you, check the transmission-fluid level first (see page 244).

If the transmission is low on fluid, add the correct type of fluid. At that time, take note of the color of the transmission fluid on the dipstick. If it smells burnt and is dark brown or black, you can expect major transmission repairs. If it is light colored, either red or greenish, the problem might be less complicated.

Two: Many older cars and some newer cars have a device on the transmission called a modulator. This device is mounted on the transmission and must have a good engine vacuum to make the transmission work properly. If the vacuum hose is clogged or disconnected, the transmission will delay shifting or might not shift at all. Before assuming you need a major transmission repair, ask your mechanic to make sure the vacuum to the transmission modulator, if your car is so equipped, is good.

Three: The shift point—that is, the precise speed at which the transmission shifts—on most modern cars is controlled by a cable. If the cable is broken, disconnected, or misadjusted, the transmission might not shift properly. Have your mechanic check the cable.

Four: It might be possible for the transmission-shift selector linkage to be misaligned or even disconnected. Often the point indicating which gear you are in is not synchronized with the actual transmission gear into which the selector has placed the transmission. Before agreeing to major repairs, have your mechanic check the transmission linkage for disconnected, bent, or broken parts.

Transmission Slips or Jerks (Automatic)

Symptoms

Normally you really don't feel the gear shifts that occur with your automatic transmission unless you're really trying. Then suddenly one day you begin noticing a very definite change in feel or sound as the automatic transmission changes gears. After a while there might even be a momentary loss of pulling power or a jerk at about fifteen miles per hour. There might be another hesitation or jerk at about twenty-five miles per hour. You might also find that when you slow down and try to accelerate, there is hesitation when the car jerks ahead.

Explanation

The automatic transmission depends on hydraulic pressure to apply a series of clutches that create first, second, third, and fourth gears, and reverse. When everything is working normally, a system of valves senses the vehicle speed and load and directs hydraulic pressure to activate the various gears. When pressure is low things don't work the way they should. A loss of transmission fluid can allow air to get into the hydraulic system, and more problems can arise. So the first place to look for a transmission problem is the fluid level. A slip or jerk—that is, when the transmission suddenly stops transmitting power to the rear wheels—occurs when pressure is lost (also see page 168).

Diagnoses and Solutions

One: As in all transmission-related problems, the first thing to do is check the transmission-fluid level (see page 244). A low transmission-fluid level can cause any of the symptoms previously described. If you find that refilling the transmission corrects the problem, have the cause of the transmission-fluid loss corrected as soon as possible.

> **CAUTION: Left unrepaired, a transmission operated on low fluid will eventually self-destruct.**

Two: If the transmission-fluid level is at the full mark, the cause of jerking, bucking, and slippage between shifts becomes more involved. First and foremost, on newer cars, is the adjustment of the cable between the throttle and the transmission. This is called a TV cable on many cars. It is the device used to inform the transmission of the amount of throttle you are demanding. When it goes out of adjustment on many cars, the transmission can stay in low gear or jerk. On older cars, similar symptoms occur when there is a problem with the vacuum supply to a device called a transmission modulator. Ask your mechanic about these devices before agreeing to a transmission rebuild.

Three: If the transmission TV cable or modulator is okay, the next step is to seek out the service of a competent mechanic who will perform a transmission-pressure test to determine the cause of the problem.

Four: In some cases the transmission filter becomes clogged and causes a loss of power, hesitation, and even a slippage between gears. Usually this condition will be accompanied by a loud whining sound coming from under the car in the area of the transmission. The whining sound will increase as the car is accelerated. Have the transmission fluid and filter replaced, and try again.

> **CAUTION:** If the transmission fluid has a strong burnt odor and is dark brown or black, don't expect that a simple adjustment will correct the problem. Once the transmission fluid burns, odds are that your entire automatic transmission will have to be rebuilt.

Engine Runs, but Car Will Not Move (Automatic)

Symptoms

You start the engine normally and shift the automatic-transmission gear selector to the drive position. You step on the gas and the engine runs faster, but the car does not move forward.

Explanation

Most modern automatic transmissions are hydraulic, which means they depend on transmission fluid. The fluid is pumped under pressure to make the various clutches apply and release. Fluid is used to control the moment when the transmission shifts gears. When the transmission leaks and you lose fluid, the remaining transmission fluid can become aerated. Air in the transmission fluid can cause the transmission to slip and jump. It is very important to check the transmission fluid at least once a month. If you find a loss of transmission fluid, have your mechanic check for a transmission-fluid leak (see page 168).

Diagnoses and Solutions

One: Shift into low gear and see if the car moves forward. Next try the same thing with the shift selector in the D, D1, or D2 position. If the car moves forward in other positions but not in the normal drive, your problem might simply be a misadjusted shift-lever position indicator. You might also find that when the shift indicator points to neutral your car is actually in reverse. Try carefully accelerating in neutral to see if the car moves backward. If the car moves in reverse when the indicator points to neutral and goes forward only in D1 or D2, the problem is most likely a shift-indicator malfunction. Repairing a malfunctioning shift indicator is a relatively simple job and can be done by most mechanics.

Two: If the car moves neither forward nor back in any of the shift positions, the problem might be a loss of transmission fluid. On most automatic transmissions you must check the fluid level with the transmission shift selector in the park position and the engine running. Be sure to set the parking brake. Locate the transmission-fluid dipstick. If you can't find it, check the owner's manual for its location. Remove the dipstick and take a look at the end. There are markings that indicate when the transmission is full; generally there are crossed lines indicating the proper level. If the fluid line is below these crossed lines, the transmission is low on fluid. When an automatic transmission has lost most of its fluid, the transmission will slip and the car might not move either forward or in reverse. If there is no evidence of transmission fluid on the dipstick, add a quart and recheck the stick. It will probably take three or four quarts to put the level where it belongs. Once you have refilled the transmission to its proper level, try shifting into drive to see if the car now moves forward.

Three: If you find the car will move in reverse but not forward, or if it only moves forward and you cannot get it to move in reverse, chances are there is serious internal trouble in the transmission, which will require the services of a transmission mechanic.

Four: If the car still doesn't move after you have filled the transmission-fluid reservoir and you hear a loud whining from under the car, the transmission-fluid filter might be clogged. A clogged transmission filter will keep the car from moving. Have your mechanic check for a clogged filter. A new filter and fluid may help, but you will probably need major repairs soon even if replacing the filter gets the car moving.

CAUTION: Driving a car with a transmission low on fluid might cause costly premature damage to the transmission. If you discover that you are low on transmission fluid, have the transmission fluid refilled as soon as possible.

APPENDIX

A

Safety Tips, Emergency Repair, and Basic Car Care

Driving to Prolong the Life of Your Car

The way you drive your car can make a great deal of difference in the number of years your car lasts. It can also make a difference in the total amount of money you will spend just to keep it going for as long as you own it. Some of the very basic things you do when driving your car might be taking a major toll in the way of premature wear and tear. Let's begin with the way you start your car on a cold morning. Many drivers listen to the morning news and decide their engine needs extra time to warm up. So, they throw on a coat, start the engine, and then go back inside the house to have breakfast. Prolonged warmup periods will make your car nice and warm when you finally get into it, but you will have caused unnecessary wear and tear on your engine. During the warmup period, all sorts of contamination is created in the engine. Your best bet is to get into your car, start the engine, buckle your seat belts, and then shift into gear and drive off. Avoid any rapid acceleration for the first few blocks while the engine is coming up to operating temperature. Remember that your engine will warm up sooner if you drive your car than it will idling in the driveway.

Rapid acceleration is always a strain on the engine and transmission. It doesn't do the tires, drive axles, and motor mounts any good either. When you step on the gas pedal, extra quantities of fuel are sprayed into the intake manifold. This extra fuel mixture uses more fuel and causes the engine to work harder. The sudden increase in power or torque strains the moving parts of the engine, causes the engine to twist against the motor mounts, strains the transmission, and punishes the differential. You are far better off accelerating gently and bringing the car up to the desired speed at a slower rate. You really don't save much time flooring the accelerator pedal, but you do cause a great deal more wear. In addition to wear, rapid acceleration makes for a very uncomfortable ride for your passengers. Every time you slam down on the gas pedal your passengers are thrown backward. You might not notice the movement because you are holding onto the steering wheel. Be assured it is very uncomfortable for your passengers when you accelerate rapidly. There is also the safety factor to consider. If the road is slippery or your tires are worn, you stand a far greater chance of losing traction at the driving wheels if you floor the gas pedal.

The same drivers who drive in what is known as jackrabbit style are often also the same drivers who do a lot more braking than is necessary. If you accelerate rapidly, you often have to jam on the brakes to avoid a situation you have driven into at too fast a rate of speed. Every time you brake you wear off some of the brake pads and lining. The more often you brake, the quicker the brakes wear out. In addition, if you brake too often, the brakes overheat. This overheating can cause reduced braking power, rapid brake wear, and eventual damage to the disc-brake rotors and rear brake drums. Also, your passengers are thrown forward when you brake suddenly. One good way to reduce brake wear is to anticipate your stops. Let's say, for example, you are rolling along on the interstate at fifty-five miles per hour. You see a sign that the toll booth is just a quarter mile ahead. Some drivers just roll right along until they are within stopping distance, then take their foot off the gas and begin braking. The smart driver anticipates that he will be stopping soon and reduces his speed gradually as he or she approaches the toll booth. The idea is to keep the car rolling but allow it to slow down normally without braking until the last minute, when you need to brake to stop. This same technique should be used for parkway exits or for when you are approaching slowed traffic. You certainly don't want to slow down to a crawl in the passing lane, but you can effectively reduce the amount of braking by simply slowing down sooner and using less power. Over the life of your car, this type of driving will save you money in reduced fuel consumption and reduced wear and tear.

Making a turn at a higher rate of speed than is necessary will also cause premature tire wear and put extra strain on the steering and suspension components. High-speed turns also make your passengers less comfortable and increase the risk of a skid when you encounter slippery pavement. At slower speeds you are in more control of your car and are in a better position to steer out of a problem than you would be when roaring through a turn at higher speeds.

One of the best demonstrations of the proper techniques for a sensible driver comes from veteran race-car driver Jackie Stewart. In his videotape "Behind the Wheel with Jackie Stewart" (Karl-Lorimar Home Video, 17942 Cowan, Irvine, CA 92714), he tapes a large plastic dish to the hood of his car. Then he places a rubber ball in the dish. The idea is to accelerate, decelerate, stop, and turn the car without having the rubber ball roll out of the plastic dish. To make it through the course of traffic cones Jackie Stewart has set up for the demonstration, a driver has to accelerate gently, decelerate gently, anticipate the stops and turns, and nego- tiate them carefully. In other words, all of these techniques make for a smooth drive and provide a good, safe, and com- fortable ride for your passengers. A jackrabbit start would obviously send the rubber ball careening out of the dish. So would a sudden stop or too fast a turn. Although it might not be practical for you to do what Jackie Stewart does to demonstrate sensible driving techniques, it might be a good idea for you to imagine the dish and ball set up on your hood. Try to drive as if you had the same plastic dish taped to the hood of your car. You will soon be driving in a much smarter, safer, and more economical way.

This is true of both local city driving and highway driving. If your present method of taking curves or your stopping or starting would send the ball out of the dish, your driving technique needs some work. You can start practicing the next time you drive your car. You will reduce the wear and tear on your car, and your passengers will surely appreciate a smooth ride.

How to Go in the Snow

Even the mere forecast of snow strikes terror into the hearts of some drivers. I, for one, enjoy the snow because it brings a different dimension to driving. It is sort of like fighting with one hand tied behind your back. The secret to safe driving in snow, ice, and even rain is to be prepared for the various driving conditions these materials present. Obviously snow is slippery, and it will reduce the grip your tires have on the road. This means, first and foremost, that you cannot stop quickly on ice or snow. Nor can you accelerate rapidly. You also cannot expect to turn the car in the same way you can on a normally dry road. Remember that the tires are not going to grip the road surface when there is a layer of snow, ice, or even rain between the road and the tire treads.

Rule number one when you drive on snow or ice is to slow down. When you drive on snow or ice, think of your vehicle as operating more like a boat than a car. On dry pavement, the tires grip and you move off in a straight line because the power is transmitted evenly to the two or four driving wheels. The front tires, on the steering wheels, grip and keep the car going straight. On ice and snow, the driving wheels slip until they can get some traction. This means that only a fraction of the actual power that would normally move the car is committed to moving the car forward. The tires don't grip, so the wheels spin faster, making it even more difficult for them to grip the road. When you are on ice or snow, apply the gas very lightly. Do not allow the tires to spin wildly in the hope that they will suddenly grip the road through the snow or ice. What actually happens when you allow them to spin is that they polish the ice and pack the snow, making it even more difficult to gain traction.

If you're stuck in snow or ice, you can use sand, gravel, cat litter, dirt, or any similar substance to give the driving wheels extra traction. Throw the sand toward the front of the two driving wheels (the front wheels on front-wheel-drive cars, the rear wheels on others). Sand a little path ahead of the tires to be sure the traction is good for at least a few feet. There are mats made for the purpose of providing extra traction for cars stuck on snow or ice. These will work very well, provided you accelerate slowly.

> **CAUTION: Do not allow anyone to stand in the rear of the car. I once witnessed a driver trying to free his car from a snowdrift using these mats. He placed the two steel mats just ahead of the rear wheels. He gunned the engine, and one of the mats flew out from the rear of the car and hit his son, who was standing behind the car. The boy suffered severe cuts to the face when the mat went flying (and the car remained stuck in the snow).**

Just as the tires cannot grip to accelerate in snow or ice, the front, steering tires cannot grip well to make the car turn. The front tires have to grip the road to change the direction in which the car is driving. When there is a slippery substance between the tire tread and the road, the turning tires slip. The car does not respond as quickly or as accurately to your turning the steering wheel. When you want the car to turn, it tends to go straight. If there is a crown in the road, the car tends to drift toward the lower side of the crown. On a three-lane highway, for example, try to stay in the center lane, as far as possible from the low sides of the crown. This will help keep your car from becoming a downhill skier.

Rule two is to keep your steering movements to a minimum. If you are stuck in the snow, keep the wheels straight ahead until you feel the car rolling under control. If the wheels are turned to the left or right as you are trying to gain traction, you are providing more resistance to the movement of the car. Keep the wheels straight ahead so that they can roll with the least amount of resistance.

These same concepts apply to braking in snow or ice. For a car to stop on dry pavement, the tires must grip the road as the brakes stop the wheels from rotating. If you brake harshly on snow or ice, the wheels instantly stop turning and the car begins to slide. The bottom part of the tire, which is making actual contact with the road, becomes a sort of ski. When you jam on the brakes you are no longer driving; you're going along for a ski ride in the snow.

The secret to stopping in the snow is to gently pump the brakes, allowing some time for the wheels to roll freely so that you can gain steering traction and slow the forward movement of the car. This, incidentally, is the theory on which antilock braking systems work. When you jam on the brakes in an antilock system, the system automatically pumps the brakes to allow the tires to gain a grip on the road.

> **CAUTION: Remember the third rule: Never, never, never jam down on the brake pedal in snow or ice. You will surely lock the brakes and very likely put the car into an uncontrollable skid.**

The secret to driving in snow or ice is to go slowly, steer sparingly, and anticipate your stops. You simply cannot drive the same on ice or snow as you can on dry pavement. Snow tires, tire chains, or all-season tires are a must for snow and ice. Four-wheel drive, antilock brakes, and the new traction-control systems are great advantages in adverse weather, but don't assume, even with these systems, that you can drive as if there were no snow or ice. One of the great mistakes four-wheel-drive owners make is assuming they can travel in any ice or snow at the same speeds they would in dry weather. This is simply not the case. Four-wheel-drive vehicles can slip and slide and go out of control just like any other vehicle. They are indeed better than a normal car, but they are not invincible.

Suppose you follow all of the foregoing rules but still suddenly lose control. If you are going slowly, you have less chance of doing serious damage. If you are driving fast, any damage that occurs is to be expected. However, let's say you suddenly feel the rear of the car moving toward your left. Do not jam on the brakes. Do not fully release your foot from the gas pedal. Do back off on the gas, but keep some power applied to the wheels. Steer in the direction you want the car to go. Do not cut the wheels to the full right or left position. Steer gently, maintaining some forward movement if it is safe to do so.

There are some additional precautions you should take to make your driving in snow or ice safer and more enjoyable. Buy a set of wiper blades made specially for use in snow. These blades have a special rubber covering that keeps them from freezing in snow or icy rain. They are well worth the money, because they will keep on working long after conventional blades have frozen and can no longer clear the snow or rain from the windshield. Buy an inexpensive plastic toolbox and fill it with some items that might come in handy in snow conditions. Here is a partial list:

- clean work gloves
- roll of duct tape
- small roll of wire
- pliers
- screwdriver
- flashlight
- road flares
- matches
- cans of dry roasted peanuts or other nonperishable food
- candles
- empty coffee can
- plastic bag for carrying water
- electrical tape
- adjustable wrench
- jumper cables
- snow brush
- tire inflator
- extra fuses

Be sure you take along plenty of warm clothing, even if the weather is fairly nice; it might get colder later in the day. Buy a snow shovel or an army-surplus entrenching tool to dig yourself out of snow drifts. Buy two bags of builder's sand and keep them in the trunk, providing additional weight for extra traction, or throw some sand under the tires should you get stuck. If your travels in snow take you through isolated areas where it might be possible that you could be stranded for a long time, take along these items:

- thermal blanket (for each person)
- first-aid kit
- coil of rope
- portable winch
- tow cable
- portable CB radio
- cellular phone

These last items sound like elaborate protection, but they are not. Every winter you read of people getting stranded in the snow. Just a few years ago two people were caught in an avalanche that buried their car with snow. They lived for nearly two weeks on dried foods, such as peanuts, they had brought along. They drank melted snow and kept warm bundled up in parkas and bedrolls they had brought along for camping. Finally they were missed and someone sent a rescue team to dig them out. Had they told a friend where they were going and when they were expected to arrive, the rescue alert would have probably started much sooner. Make up a travel plan and tell a friend or relative what you are doing. Arrange to check in from time to time, with the understanding that if you aren't heard from, it could be because you are stuck in the snow. It is entirely possible to be stranded in snow within a mile of a highly populated area. When you roll toward the side of the road, there is always a chance that your car could be hidden from view. Plan ahead to have someone alert the police if your arrival is delayed. Make sure they know where you will be traveling and about what time.

Driving in the snow can be safe and fun if you are careful and treat it as a distinct type of driving. If you are going to drive in snow just as you would on dry pavement, all bets are off and you're on your own.

Driving in the Rain

When you drive a car, there is an almost reflex warning system that sounds when you realize it has begun to rain. You know that unless you switch on the wipers, the droplets of rainwater falling on your windshield will soon prevent you from clearly seeing the road. Once you switch on the wipers, your vision is nearly normal, provided the wiper blades are in good condition. Notice, I said "nearly normal." In fact, water on the windshield reduces your vision, but you can still see well enough to drive.

What far too many motorists fail to realize is that a tire's ability to grip the road is also reduced in rain. The rainwater on the road does two things. First, it acts as a lubricant between the road surface and the tread on your tires. Second, rain lifts oil, grease, and bits of ground-off rubber that have sunk into the pores of the road surface. The combination of rainwater, oil, grease, and rubber creates a barrier that prevents your tires from fully gripping the road. Remember that the tire tread must actually grip the road for you to accelerate, turn, and stop. Perhaps the best analogy is to compare driving on a rainy day with driving on a dry day after someone has thoroughly covered all four tires with a thick layer of heavy grease.

No matter how good your tires are—no matter if they are all-season tires, snow tires, rain tires, or even tractor tires— they simply cannot grip the road as well when there is a layer of water between them and the road. That is a fact of life that must be remembered whenever you drive any car with or without four-wheel drive, all-wheel drive, traction control, antilock brakes, rear-wheel or front-wheel drive. At speeds under thirty-five miles per hour, the grip of your tires is good in even the worst rain. Remember that it is still not nearly as good as it would be on a dry road. So, even at slow speeds, you have to be far more careful to avoid sudden stops, sudden turns, and sudden acceleration. Any of these can easily break your tires' grip on the road when the road surface is wet.

Above thirty-five miles per hour, and depending on the type of tire and car you drive, another phenomenon can occur. Above thirty-five miles per hour, when the water conditions on the road ahead are just right and you're driving as if it weren't raining, your car can begin to hydroplane. When the conditions are just right, a layer of water gets between the surface of the road and the bottom of your tires. The tires are kept from gripping the road and your car begins to hydroplane. It is a little like skimming a rock across a pond. The tire stays on top of the thin layer of water and does not grip the road surface. The result is that the car cannot be steered, stopped, or turned normally. When you're hydroplaning you're out of control. It can happen at any moment when you drive too fast for the water conditions on the road surface.

When it starts raining and you reach for the wiper switch, you should also switch yourself into a slower, much more cautious driving mode. Do not drive at the full speed limit when it is raining. If it is raining harder, drive slower. If the rain becomes blinding, pull off the road where it is safe to do so and wait for the rain to slacken. Don't be intimidated or encouraged to drive faster by those motorists who seem to drive just as fast and no more cautiously in the rain. You must slow down in the rain if you are going to maintain safe control of your car. Improvements such as four-wheel or all-wheel drive, antilock brakes, traction control, all-season and rain tires are truly wonderful. However, they are only safety aids. They are not designed to turn a wet road into a dry road. When the road is wet, these devices will help and might save you from a serious accident or injury, but don't depend on them to supplement good judgment.

Factor in speed, braking, and the effects of your car's momentum and its tendency to keep moving in one direction despite your efforts to stop it or steer it, and you can see the reason for some hard and fast rules about driving in the rain.

Slow down and steer as little as possible to avoid getting the car off course. Accelerate slowly and imagine there is a raw egg between your foot and the accelerator pedal; drive as if you were trying to keep from breaking the raw egg. Use your brakes sparingly, allowing time for the wheels to keep rolling and steering and time for slowing the car. Anticipate your stops and take your foot off the gas to allow the car's own engine to slow it down without your braking. Stop firmly but gently. Don't jam down hard on the brakes, unless you have absolutely no other choice. A sudden panic stop on a wet surface can put your car into an uncontrollable spin or skid. Finally, when you drive in the rain, look for escape routes you can follow when you come to a stop. Leave more room on a rainy day to stop. Give yourself enough time to avoid a driver ahead who might have locked up his brakes in a panic stop.

In short, you have to learn to drive differently when it rains. The main rule is always slow down when it rains.

Don't Drive on the Autumn Leaves

Autumn beckons to drivers to seek out those back roads where the full beauty and majesty of the blaze of colors can be best appreciated. Plan your fall leaf-watching excursions early and be careful about driving over or parking on autumn leaves. Leaves have a tendency to maintain moisture long after the rest of the road surface is dry. What might look like an innocent pile of leaves might be hiding a slippery surface on which your car will slide if you attempt to stop. If the pile of leaves is on a turn or where you need to stop, attempting to brake on the leaves could send your car skidding out of control. Another important reason to stay off a pile of leaves is the possibility of children hiding under it. This is particularly true in residential areas. Avoid driving over what might seem like nothing more than a pile of raked autumn leaves; there could be a small child under the leaves. Finally, never park your car on a pile of autumn leaves. There have been numerous cases of the leaves actually catching fire when the leaves make contact with the extremely hot catalytic converter, which is part of the exhaust system of most modern cars.

Pulling a Trailer

You can safely pull a small utility trailer with just about any car, even a little subcompact. However, you cannot expect to pull a two-horse trailer or a speedboat trailer with a subcompact car. It makes sense to think about the car before you buy the trailer. If, for example, you have purchased an eighteen-foot speedboat with two outboard motors and a trailer, by the time you are through filling the gas tanks and filling up the food locker, you will have a pretty heavy load. There are limits to the load any car can safely handle, even with a trailering package. When you have chosen the boat or the house or the horse trailer, calculate the total gross load. That is, the horse, the hay, the saddles, the spare tire, and the trailer itself. If it is a boat trailer, you need to include the gasoline, the cushions, the fishing poles, the life preservers, the gas, the water, the ice, the water skis, and anything else you might have decided to bring along. When you have the total gross weight of the fully loaded trailer, you are ready to think about the car that will pull that trailer. Many small cars have a load limit of a thousand pounds. If your car has that type of limit, you simply cannot pull a heavy trailer. You can find out the trailering capability of your car by checking the owner's manual. If the limit isn't in the manual, call the car maker's customer-service telephone number. Some car dealers such as Chevrolet have extensive material available on trailering. Check with the car dealer for the load limits of your car and the availability of an appropriate trailer hitch.

There are several companies that make trailer hitches that will precisely fit your car. The important thing to remember is that the trailer hitch is designed to handle the maximum gross load of your trailer. Let's say your fully loaded trailer weighs fifteen hundred pounds. You can safely pull that trailer with a Class I trailer hitch. If the load you plan to pull is closer to three thousand pounds, you will need a Class II trailer hitch. When you get into heavier trailers, you might have to step up to a Class III hitch. The important thing to remember is that your trailer hitch and ball must be rated to safely carry the load you plan to pull.

TRAILER-HITCH CAPACITY

Class	Maximum Gross Load
I	2,000 lbs.
(some models go to 2,500 lbs.)	
II	3,500 lbs.
III	3,500 to 10,000 lbs.

The best type of trailer hitch to buy is one custom-designed to fit precisely your make, model, and year of car or light truck. Don't be tempted into using a trailer hitch that clamps onto your bumper. Before bumpers were made to absorb a collision at low speeds, that was a fairly safe practice. Modern cars have energy-absorbing bumpers that are built to move when hit. If you hang a trailer hitch onto that type of bumper, you can damage the bumper, and the trailer can pull the bumper out of the little shock-absorber units onto which the bumper is mounted. The best type of trailer hitch is one that bolts onto the steel rails that are part of the car's structure.

Before you choose a trailer hitch, make sure you see all of the options. Do some research and follow the recommendations of the car and trailer manufacturers.

My favorite type of trailer hitch has what is called a receiver that bolts onto the car body. The trailer ball and tongue it sits on are then fitted into the receiver. When you aren't pulling a trailer, the ball and tongue can be removed by simply pulling out a locking pin. This type of trailer hitch can generally handle more gross load than simply bolt-on-type trailer hitches.

If your trailer is heavy enough to cause the back of the car to sag down, you should consider what is known as a load-equalizing trailer hitch. This type of hitch uses the receiver mentioned previously, but in addition has two steel bars connected to the trailer with chains. When snapped into position, the two bars act as a spring between the trailer and the car. The spring action raises the front of the trailer and the back of the car. It also distributes the load to the front wheels of the car, the back wheels of the car, and all of the trailer wheels. There are also special rear springs available for many cars. These springs provide an extra lift to the back of the car to offset the added weight of the trailer.

Another problem is overheating. Often the added burden of pulling a trailer causes the engine and transmission to run hot. There are heavy-duty radiators that can be installed to help keep the engine cool during trailering. There are also transmission-cooler kits that can be installed to help keep the transmission fluid from overheating during a long, hot, uphill trailer pull. In fact, there are catalogs full of devices to make trailering easier and safer. They include antisway shock absorbers to keep the trailer running smoothly behind the car. There are special shock absorbers with air bags to raise the back of the car for trailering. Special lighting kits are made to convert your car's brake and turn-signal system to work with the trailer's lights. There are safety chains that will secure the trailer to the car in the event the trailer ball disconnects. The list is endless. The thing to do is to obtain a trailering-equipment catalog so that you know what is available to make your trailering easier.

You might find that your car is just not adequate for trailering or that you don't feel it has enough power to handle a big trailer. If that is the case, don't just buy a bigger car. Ask your dealer to suggest a car built with trailering options. In this way, you can get a new car with a heavy-duty radiator, special differential, transmission cooler, special springs, and even the trailer hitch and wiring built in at the factory. When you are looking over a car with trailering options, also ask about a sport-utility vehicle, which might actually be better suited to pull a trailer. When it comes to larger trailers, you are better off with a full-size truck than you are with any passenger car.

Regardless of what type of car or truck and trailer combination you drive, you have to learn to drive a trailer safely. You simply cannot expect to accelerate, decelerate, and stop the same way when you're pulling a trailer as you do when you are driving the same car without a trailer. You have the ever-present danger of jack-knifing. It happens so often that it should be the primary concern of any person pulling a trailer. Jack-knifing occurs more often on wet or icy roads, but it can happen on a perfectly dry road. Speed is nearly always the culprit. If you're driving slowly there is less chance of jack-knifing than if you take a turn at what might be a safe limit for the same car or truck without a trailer. Sudden panic braking sets off the jack-knifing. The car or truck stops, but the weight and momentum of the trailer keep it moving forward and to one side of the car or truck. The result can be injury to passengers and serious damage to both the trailer and the car or truck. The number-one rule when towing a trailer is to slow down. Anticipate your stops and leave double the distance between you and the car ahead. Give yourself time to react to a sudden stop ahead. Remember that there is a flexible connection between the car and the trailer. The most effective braking occurs when the trailer is directly behind the car. If it is off to the side, you have to be extremely careful when braking.

Trailers are more vulnerable to wind conditions than passenger cars or trucks. If it is extremely windy, avoid bridges and turnpikes. When you are trailering you have to learn to check the trailer tires and the trailer coupling every time you stop. I once had a mischievous teenager release my trailer-hitch lock while I was stopped for a traffic light. Had I not noticed him duck behind my car I might have lost the trailer on the highway.

If your trailer is big enough to have its own brakes, you must learn how to check them to see if they are working. You must also check the brakes just as you would the brakes on your car. Boat trailers are particularly vulnerable to rusted wheel bearings, because the rear wheels are often submerged in water during launching. Learn to take good care of your trailer and it will serve you well. Learn how to change a flat on the trailer and be equipped with a spare tire and a lug wrench that will also fit the lug nuts on your trailer wheels. Make sure your jack will also lift the trailer. If you are going on a long trip, take along an extra set of brake lamps and a spare tire for the trailer. Include an extra set of wheel bearings and seals. Trailer parts are often difficult to find and can take several days to obtain. Having a supply of spare trailer parts along could save your vacation.

When it comes to pulling a trailer, it all boils down to using good common sense along with taking the time to acquire the knowledge you need to trailer. You can learn to back up any trailer, but it takes practice. Before you set out on that adventure, find a large open area where you can set up some traffic cones and learn how to back up. The best way is by actually doing it alone. I find that when you're learning to back up a trailer, having someone around just confuses the matter. Make sure you really can't do any damage. Move slowly and try backing into an imaginary driveway created with cones or cardboard boxes. Be careful you don't jack-knife while backing up. If you get into trouble, stop the car, shut off the engine, and get out and look at the situation. You will soon figure it out. The rule is to pull ahead to get the trailer straight behind the car, and then try again. Once the trailer is off to one side or the other, it will move in that direction. Take your time, don't get excited, and don't listen to well-intentioned onlookers who probably have never tried to back up a trailer.

Good luck, and have a great time trailering.

Beware the Highwayman

A deserted stretch of highway has never been a very safe place, but in recent times we have seen more and more incidents of crime on the highway. One favorite ruse is for the modern highwayman to create an accident. Under normal circumstances you would stop, take out your wallet, and exchange license and insurance information. This puts you in an extremely vulnerable position. If you are alone and suspicious that you could become a victim of this type of scam, lock your doors and motion to the other driver to follow you to the nearest police station, toll booth, service or fire station. Keep a photocopy of your driver's license, registration, and insurance information in the glove compartment. Make a notation on the photocopy asking the other driver to follow you to the nearest police station. Open the window just enough to pass out the photocopy, and then proceed to the nearest police station. Try to make a note of the other driver's license plate so that you can properly report the incident to the authorities. One woman driver I know keeps a folded cardboard sign under the driver's seat. One side says FOLLOW

ME TO THE POLICE STATION. The other says PLEASE CALL
THE POLICE.

Are You Prepared for a Flat Tire?

You haven't had a flat tire in years; then suddenly you're
zipping along on the interstate when you hear that ominous
sound of a tire blowing out. You struggle to a safe stop off
to the side of the road and set about the task of changing
the flat tire and putting on the spare. For a great number of
drivers that may be the very first time they have actually had
to use the wheel nut wrench and jack that is so cleverly tucked
in with the spare in the dark reaches of the trunk. Or is it in
the trunk? Some minivans have the spare tire bolted to the
underside of the rear of the van; some cars have the spare
tire in the engine compartment, while most station wagons
have the spare tire hidden behind a panel in the rear of the
passenger compartment. At a time when you are already
angry about getting the flat in the first place, you are handed
the added frustration of learning how to jack up the car—
once you have actually found the jack, wheel-nut wrench,
wheel or wheel-cover lock, and of course, the spare tire.

The flimsy L-shaped wheel-nut wrenches that come with
your car are difficult for anyone to handle. Don't feel badly
if you have trouble getting the hang of just how to use it. If
you're a planner, you might invest in a good-sized wheel-nut
or lug wrench made in a cross shape. Some auto-supply stores
also have a wheel wrench that multiplies the leverage on the
wheel nut to make removing it easier. These are easier to
use and hold in place. Or you might want to treat yourself
to an electric impact wrench that plugs into the cigarette

lighter, for 12-volt power from your battery. If you're stuck with the wrench that came with your car, try loosening the wheel nuts before you fully jack up the car. Allow the weight of the car to keep the wheel from turning. Don't remove the nuts, just loosen them, then jack up the car and remove the nuts.

If your problem is that you can't turn the wheel nut because it is too tight, with the wrench in place over the nut, try banging on the wrench with a hammer or a large rock. Jarring the nut may break it loose enough for you to back it off. If you have a length of pipe, put it over the end of your wheel-nut wrench handle to gain some more leverage to break loose overly tightened wheel nuts. And, make a vow to buy a good wheel-nut lug wrench as soon as possible. (The last time I mentioned this idea, the Equipment and Tool Institute wrote me a letter complaining that it was an unsafe practice. I agree. But when your stuck on a deserted road, or on a turnpike with cars and trucks whizzing by, and you don't have any tools or help from a mechanic, a length of pipe might just do the trick, and taking a little risk might be worth it.)

One of the more frequent problems of not being able to get the wheel nut off occurs when the driver forgets where he put the special wrench needed to remove wheel-locking wheel nuts. (These are special keylike tools needed to remove either the wheel covers or one of the wheel nuts on each wheel.) You can save yourself a great deal of trouble if you are careful about these special wrenches. Keep them in a safe place, preferably in the trunk near or attached to the wheel-nut wrench. Make sure all the drivers of your car know where they are and are aware of the importance of putting the wrench back in the same place. When you are stranded on the highway without this special wrench, even the emergency road-service mechanics will have difficulty changing a flat. In some cases, they may have to tow your car. Some wheel or wheel-cover locks are more difficult to remove than others. I have had some good results using a pointed-nose locking pliers. In some cases I have had to use a chisel. There are special tool kits designed to remove most of these locks. If you have the time, you might call around to tire shops and used-car dealers to ask if they have this special tool.

Suppose you cannot remove the lug nuts, either because they are seized or because you do not have a wheel-lock key. The best thing to do is to get help from emergency road service. However, if the road you are on is not patrolled, you have only one alternative. Reinstall the wheel nuts you may have removed and drive very slowly to the nearest service facility. You will undoubtedly ruin your tire by driving on it, but the price of a tire is little to pay to get you out of a dangerous situation. Remember, drive as slowly as possible, and for as short a distance as possible, to get you to the nearest phone or service facility.

Driving on a flat tire may also damage the rim. There is some risk that the broken tire could also damage other parts of the car. Drive on a flat tire at your own risk. But weigh the risks of damage to the car against what may happen to you stranded on a highway or deserted street. Never risk your life for the price of a tire.

Getting a flat is never fun. You almost always get one when you're late for a wedding or a business meeting. Your clothes get dirty and may even be damaged. If you're a women all dressed up for a special party, you'll probably cause a run in a stocking, break a nail, and ruin your hair. If you're a man, you'll start getting angry that you have torn the knee on your new suit, imbedded grease in your hands, and taken so long to do what you thought you knew how to do with ease.

There is a way to ease the pain for you and all your friends and family members. Pick a nice warm weekend afternoon and have a flat-tire-changing party. Get all the drivers in your family to go through the motions of changing a flat tire. I mean really let even your youngest sister and your macho brother actually jack up the car and change the tire. You're never too old to learn how to change your own flat tire. I have taught grandmothers and months later have been told how the lessons worked for them when they were broken down on a deserted road at night. You will be amazed at how much fun you'll have and how much everyone will learn. I have done this and I can tell you it really works. It is better to learn in the driveway than out on the highway. You will save time and anguish for all.

How to Safely Boost a Dead Battery

Although it might seem a simple thing to attach one battery to another in order to start a car with a dead battery, most people do it incorrectly, thus putting themselves at great risk. Under the right conditions, any car battery can explode. All it takes is a spark to ignite battery gases that might have accumulated around the top of the battery. This is particularly true when the battery has just been recharged, either by your car's alternator or a separate battery charger. Make no mistake, when a battery explodes it literally explodes like a hand grenade. Pieces of the battery case, the battery plates, and battery acid suddenly burst off in all directions. I have witnessed three such battery explosions. Two occurred when the person doing the boosting attached the last of the three battery jumper-cable clamps. The third occurred when a battery charger was disconnected from the battery being charged without first switching the battery charger off. In one of the three battery explosions, the person doing the boosting suffered a serious eye injury. In the others, quick action with clean water to flush the battery acid out of the eyes and off the skin of the persons involved prevented any serious injury.

The main thing to remember in boosting any dead battery is to prevent a spark near the battery. The spark always occurs when you make the last of the four connections, which completes the circuit. Here is how you can safely boost your dead battery on any negative ground vehicle. The vast majority of modern cars are negatively ground, so unless you have a very old or unusual car you can assume it is negative ground. Untangle your jumper cables so that you have one red and one black jumper-cable clamp at one end of the set and one black and one red jumper-cable clamp at the other end. This is important, because if you are careless and wind up with two of the same color clamps at one end and two of the same color clamps at the other end of the set, you could create a dangerous short circuit and cause yourself or others injury. Most jumper-cable sets have red and black clamps. Some, however, use green clamps instead of red. The important thing to remember is that the same color (red) clamps must go on both positive terminals; the same color (black) clamps must go on both negative terminals.

Let's, as they say in the army, do it by the numbers. (1) Connect one red jumper-cable clamp to the positive (+) terminal of the discharged battery. You can tell which is the positive terminal by the plus (+) sign molded into the battery case next to the positive terminal. (2) Connect the other end of the red jumper cable to the positive (+) terminal of the fully charged battery. (3) Connect one end of the black jumper cable to the negative (−) terminal of the fully charged battery. (4) This is the most important and final connection. DO NOT MAKE THE LAST CONNECTION TO THE BATTERY. Before you attach the negative jumper-cable clamp, select a good solid part of the engine, such as a heavy steel bracket for the alternator or the exhaust manifold. Make sure the last connection is made well away from the battery. The idea is to prevent the tiny spark created during that final connection from igniting battery gases that might have accumulated on or near the battery.

You might find that the car with the discharged battery will not turn over rapidly when you simply connect the jumper cables. If this occurs, check your connections, particularly the last negative connection to the engine itself. Use the clamp to scrape through any rust or dirt, which can prevent a good connection. If you are sure the connections are good, yet the car still won't start immediately, leave the jumper cables in place and run the engine with the fully charged battery for a while. This allows the alternator from the running car to recharge the other car's dead battery. Then try to start the dead car after ten or fifteen minutes.

In some instances, attempting to start a car with a dead battery can cause the starter to jam. The starter can sometimes be released by rapping it with a hammer. This is a job for someone familiar with where to find the starter, so don't attempt it unless you have a good knowledge of automobiles and how they work. The most important lesson to learn about boosting a dead battery is the danger of explosion.

> **CAUTION:** Boosting a battery can be risky even when you do it correctly. It is possible, under certain rare conditions, for a battery to explode without your doing anything wrong. For this reason, keep children away from the cars you are attempting to boost or whenever you are working near a battery. Provide adequate ventilation. Wear eye protection, and above all remember that all it takes is a spark to cause a battery to explode.

Before You Call for a Tow Truck

No matter how careful you are about maintaining your car, there is always the possibility, for one reason or another, that you will not be able to bring your car home under its own power. You might pick up a load of dirty or watery gasoline from a gas station whose tanks were contaminated during a flood or heavy rain. Your ignition system might fail. Your engine could seize. You could break a timing belt. The possibilities are numerous.

At some time you will probably need to be towed. It is important to know how your car should be towed. Once the tow truck, also called a wrecker, is on the scene, it is too late to do much about exactly what type of tow truck will move your car.

The basic type of tow truck, and probably the type you have seen most often, uses steel cables and a heavy metal bar. In addition to the bar, there might also be wide, rubber-covered slings. The bar hooks onto your bumper with chains, and either the front or rear of the car is raised off the ground. This is a very primitive form of tow truck. It is actually obsolete, because all modern cars have energy-absorbing bumpers. If you lift the car by its bumper you stand a chance of damaging the energy-absorbing devices. The hooks and chains used to attach the car to the large steel bar have to be hooked to the suspension of the car. An experienced tow truck operator, who takes the time to be careful, can safely hook up many cars provided he uses the special chains and blocks various cars require. However, there are some cars that should never be towed by the bumpers, no matter how eager or experienced the tow man.

The only safe way in which some cars should be lifted for towing is by the wheels. There are very special vehicles called wheel-lift tow trucks, which actually lift the car by its wheels and tires. Special frames are used to clamp around the base of the front or rear tires. This puts no strain on the frame of the car. All of the car's weight is on its wheels, just as it would be when the car is rolling down the highway. The wheel-lift method eliminates the possibility of damage from chains and hooks.

The chains with large J-shaped hooks are used to secure the car to a more conventional towing-truck bar. It is easy for them to cause damage to the front or rear under part of the car. For example, it is possible for a towing hook to tear through the soft rubber boot coverings of a front-drive axle's constant-velocity joint. If undetected, this type of damage could cause the drive-axle joints to wear prematurely. The front axles might then need to be replaced. There is also the possibility of major and costly damage to the body and frame of certain cars. It is possible to incorrectly tow a car such as a fiberglass-bodied Corvette and cause damage that might cost several thousand dollars to repair. The windshield might crack on some cars that are lifted incorrectly.

When any car with an automatic transmission is towed, certain precautions must be taken to prevent damage. Your owner's manual should be checked to find out precisely what limits there are on how far and how fast your car can be towed with either the front or rear wheels on the ground. In some instances, rear-wheel-drive cars might need to have the drive shaft disconnected before being towed a long distance. It is much more difficult, and more than likely impractical, to disconnect the drive axles on front-wheel-drive cars.

Before you break down, it is wise to check your owner's manual to find out how your particular car should be towed. There are very specific suggestions put out annually by car makers. Some cars can be towed using the old bar style or sling method, provided special wood blocks are used. In some cases the car maker might say that the front of the car can be lifted using a wheel-lift wrecker but not the rear. It is important to know what your car requires when you call for the wrecker. If you have an exotic sports car, there are generally very specific rules from the car maker on just how the car can be safely towed. Take the time to find out what those rules are by checking your owner's manual.

If you can't find the precise information in the owner's manual, ask your dealer. If that doesn't work and you can't get the maker's customer-service department to help you, there is a manual available from the American Automobile Association, which is really intended for professional tow-truck operators. It covers just about every car on the road and provides detailed information on the safest way to tow the car.

What do you do if you don't know the safest way to tow your car? There is one method that is really your best assurance that no damage will come to your car as a result of towing. It is called the flatbed truck. This flatbed, sometimes called a roll back, is really a giant platform mounted on the back of a truck. When your car needs to be towed, the tow man backs the flatbed up to your car and lowers the bed of the truck. It actually rolls back, then tilts to form a ramp onto which your disabled car is pulled using a powerful winch. Once the car is on the bed, the entire thing, car and all, is pulled back into position on top of the truck chassis. When it is chained in place, your car is as safe and protected from road damage as it would be if it were parked in your driveway. Whenever possible, try to have your car towed using a flatbed wrecker.

Before you agree to have your car towed, always find out what type of towing device is required from your car maker and insist that it be used. Once the car is unhooked from the tow truck, there is really very little chance that you will notice any damage until it is too late to recover the cost. It is better to avoid the damage in the first place by knowing how your car should be towed.

How to Deal with Your Mechanic

After the evils of doctors and lawyers, one of the favorite topics of conversation seems to be auto mechanics. Certainly there is no denying there are ripoff mechanics and even organized sales strategies designed to separate car owners from their hard-earned dollars. The trick is to find the honest, competent mechanic just like you find the honest, competent lawyer or doctor. A good place to start is by asking your friends. It is particularly true of independent mechanics that they simply don't last too long in business if they are not doing a reasonably good job, honestly and at a fair price. For this reason, it is a safe bet that if the mechanic you are considering has been in business at the same location for a number of years, you are headed in the right direction. However, even if you are highly recommended to a particular auto-repair shop, don't go and throw yourself on the mechanic's mercy. Ask about the cost of the repairs you want before you agree to have the job done. In most cases the mechanic can give you a pretty good idea of how much the job will cost. Ask for a written estimate listing the parts (with brand names specified), labor, and all other charges.

Getting a written estimate for an exhaust replacement, tires, a tuneup, brake adjustment, or any of the common repair problems is a reasonable request. Honest mechanics will have no problem providing you with a written authorization for routine jobs. However, when it comes to a repair in which the mechanic actually doesn't know what he will find until he has done some disassembly or testing, it is unreasonable to expect a written estimate before the mechanic has done an initial inspection. Ask the mechanic how much the testing or disassembly will cost and get it in writing before you agree to the work. Many jobs involving electrical short circuits or intermittent engine failure can take many hours to solve. If that is your condition, establish a dollar limit with your mechanic beyond which he will not go without your written approval.

Understand what you are getting into before you sign on the dotted line. One of the major areas of dispute between mechanics and car owners is that the mechanic failed to make it clear to the car owner that a particular job might cost several hundred dollars. Often the customer is equally at fault because he or she failed to ask for the total cost. Most often problems arise when there is a failure to communicate.

When the job is routine, make sure you get an estimate and instruct the mechanic to call you before any unauthorized work is performed. If the mechanic does call to tell you he has found an additional problem, don't assume he is dishonest and trying to pad the bill. You have the right to say no and seek a second opinion. If you don't really trust the mechanic, it might serve as a good test of his honesty. If a second opinion verifies that what he says is true, you know he is doing the job right. All too often car owners become suspicious when a mechanic tells them about other needed work. The fact is that any good mechanic will always keep his eyes open for potential trouble. If his reward for carefully checking your car is to be thought of as dishonest, you are losing out on a skill that could save you serious trouble.

Suppose you went to your doctor complaining about a skin rash and during the examination he discovered that you had high blood pressure. Wouldn't you be grateful that he was conscientious enough to take your blood pressure? The same is true of a mechanic who checks your brakes when he does a lubrication or crosses the tires. If you react badly every time a mechanic tells you that he has found a defect on your car, he will be less likely the next time to tell you about problems that might cause you a breakdown.

It is the wise car owner who develops a good relationship with a mechanic. An honest, competent mechanic who is concerned about you as a person is a good friend to have. Even if you have a relatively new car with some warranty left, it is very handy to have a mechanic whom you know and trust to help you through the problems.

Don't make the mistake some car owners do in assuming that mechanics are generally not too bright or they wouldn't be working on cars in the first place. Fortunately for the car-owning public, there are thousands of auto mechanics who really know their job and do a great job all day, every day.

The fact is that they are mechanics because they love the work. They aren't interested in being bank executives, insurance salesmen, lawyers, doctors, or any of the things that many people find very interesting. They are bright, intelligent people doing a very complicated job under very difficult conditions. When you fully understand how difficult the work of repairing automobiles really is, you will probably find a greater respect for mechanics. That respect comes more quickly for some people when they're caught in a situation in which the intelligence and skill of a single mechanic makes the difference between having a vacation or spending the best part of their time off waiting to get their car repaired. Treat your mechanic with the same respect you treat your doctor, lawyer, dentist, or stock broker. When you get behind the wheel of your car, in many ways your life is in the hands and skill of your mechanic.

Ten Questions for Your Mechanic

Does your auto mechanic really know what he is doing? Are you trusting the repair of your car to a well-meaning but outdated mechanic? With each model year, cars become increasingly more complex. Onboard computer systems control fuel injection, ignition, antilock brakes, climate control, and even suspension. Yet there is a serious shortage of people trained to diagnose and repair computerized systems. A mechanic might be terrific at repairing conventional brakes yet know nothing about antilock brakes. Another might have thirty years' experience rebuilding carburetors and still be unable to diagnose a fuel-injection problem.

Happily, there is a growing number of dedicated auto-repair technicians who have the necessary understanding of car-computer electronics, the hands-on experience, the specialized testing equipment, and the willingness to put in the time it takes to accurately diagnose state-of-the-art cars. The difficulty for a car owner is to determine if the mechanic he or she chooses is skilled enough for a particular job. Skilled professionals will generally be able to explain computer-related problems in simple terms. The impostors often offer answers that reveal their true ignorance. When questioned by a car owner as to why a yellow warning light was glowing on the instrument panel, one phony responded, "Well, sir, this here car has a big black box filled with silly cones that runs the whole shebang. When them cones get fouled up the engine just don't run right anymore. Best thing is to yank the bulb out of the warning light and forget it."

Here then are ten questions to ask your mechanic. The mechanic's answers can provide insight into his or her ability to repair the problem.

1. How do you get my car's computer to tell you what's wrong? Skilled mechanics will connect your car's computer to either a handheld or console-type machine that will command your car's computer to reveal the problems it has detected. These problems are presented in the form of trouble code numbers. To find the problem, the mechanic must follow a step-by-step series of tests suggested by the car manufacturer for each separate trouble code. A mechanic must have the testing equipment, detailed repair manuals, and know-how to use them before being allowed to touch an onboard computer system.

2. What does it mean when a car fails a state exhaust-emission test with high levels of HC and CO? HC is short for hydrocarbon. CO is carbon monoxide. Increased levels of these air-polluting gases in the exhaust might be caused by anything from a clogged air filter, the need for a tuneup, a dislodged ignition wire, or a worn-out engine to a bad onboard computer. Before entrusting the correction of this type of air-polluting and fuel-wasting condition, be sure the mechanic can explain HC and CO. Also be sure he has an exhaust-gas analyzer in use. Without this expensive equipment, there is no way a mechanic can even begin to correct exhaust-emission problems.

3. What is happening when my brake pedal pulses as I step on it? It does not require a knowledge of onboard computers for a mechanic to diagnose and repair most brake problems, unless those problems have to do with antilock-braking systems. An experienced brake mechanic should tell you that a pulsing brake pedal is generally caused by a rotor thickness variation or warped front brake rotors. He should suggest resurfacing the rotors on a brake lathe if the rotors are thick enough or replacing them.

4. Is there a way to make sure all of my engine's cylinders are working efficiently? The best way to test your engine is for the mechanic to run it through a series of tests on a computerized engine analyzer. These costly machines quickly measure each cylinder's efficiency during a cylinder power-balance test and provide a printed report listing deficiencies and their likely cause. Don't assume that every car dealer or independent mechanic has this equipment. Ask to see it and a sample computer-printed diagnostic report.

5. What could cause an automatic transmission to slip when it shifts gears? A good mechanic should first check the level of the transmission fluid and smell it to see if it has burned, indicating major wear. The mechanic should check for disconnected or misadjusted linkage. Assuming the engine is running okay, the next step would be pressure tests to find out if the transmission needs a minor repair or a complete overhaul.

6. Why would my steering wheel be difficult to move sometimes? Experienced mechanics would probably ask if the steering wheel is difficult to turn in both directions, and if the condition is worse on cold mornings. Before suggesting a costly repair, the mechanic must first check the power-steering-pump belt tension and the power-steering fluid level. The complete system should be checked for leaks. Then a power-steering-pump pressure test should be performed.

7. *Why do some mechanics wear ASE shoulder patches?* The ASE patch and its companion diploma certify that a mechanic has voluntarily taken and passed a series of tough tests given by the National Institute for Automotive Service Excellence. Although ASE certification is not a guarantee that a mechanic is honest or competent, it does prove that he has spent time and money learning his trade and that he is serious about being good at his job.

8. *My car air conditioner needs to be recharged with refrigerant gas twice a year. Is there a way to find the leak?* A skilled mechanic would agree that aside from damaging the earth's ozone layer, the loss of R-12 refrigerant is a costly nuisance. He should suggest that every part of the air conditioner be tested for leaks using an electronic leak detector. Finding a slow leak can be tedious and might require that the car be left for several hours.

9. *What is an engine internal-combustion leak and how do you find it?* An experienced mechanic should ask if you have noticed a loss of coolant or a steamy white exhaust. These are the external signs of an internal-combustion leak, most often caused by a leaking cylinder-head gasket or a cracked engine block. Exhaust gases leak from the cylinders into the cooling system. The easiest test is for the mechanic to use a device that attaches to the radiator and passes air from the radiator through a blue test liquid. If the liquid turns yellow, it proves there is an internal-combustion leak. Other tests require the removal of the fan belts and thermostat, or pressure testing each cylinder.

10. What is the difference between a four-wheel or total alignment and the type of front-wheel alignment I am used to getting on my old car? For years rear-wheel-drive cars that were not involved in a major collision generally only needed to have the front wheels aligned to provide good steering and tire wear. Newer front-wheel-drive and import cars now require that all four wheels be aligned, using costly four-wheel-alignment equipment operated by mechanics who understand how to adjust the rear wheels to follow directly behind the front wheels at the correct angles.

Car Problems Don't Cure Themselves

Many car owners like to think of their car as they might a pet. I have often heard people refer to their car as "he" or "she," or give it some special name, such as Betsy or Gus. The fact that many car owners actually buy treats for their car in the form of unneeded oil or gasoline additives is well known among mechanics. Having a special fondness for your car can be a good thing if it motivates you to provide the maintenance good car care requires. It can be a bad thing, however, if you begin to think of your car as a living thing. If your cat or dog gets sick, a good meal and some rest very often cures the problem. This is not the case with an automobile. When a noise or other symptom develops, it demands your attention. Cars do not cure themselves. If you allow a squealing noise, for example, to go unrepaired in the hope that it will cure itself, you risk a breakdown from a broken alternator belt. If your transmission starts to slip and you say a little prayer that it will be okay but don't even bother to check the transmission-fluid level, you risk unnecessary and costly damage. A leak at the rear transmission seal might cost fifty dollars to repair. Left unrepaired, the transmission fluid will continue to leak, allowing the transmission to slip and burn the clutch plates. Waiting for a transmission slip to cure itself by some miracle could cost a thousand dollars.

The same is true of performance problems. If the car is difficult to start, a failure to have it checked could lead to premature starter wear and contamination of the catalytic converter. Whenever you start a cold engine it takes a few moments for the oil pressure to properly lubricate the bearings. If the car is difficult to start, all that cold cranking takes its toll on the engine. If your battery goes dead, find out why. If you haven't left the lights on and the alternator-charge indicator shows that the alternator is charging, simply re-charging a dead battery or replacing it is not the answer. You must find out why the battery went dead in the first place.

It is perfectly all right to give your car tender loving care, but don't make the mistake of believing that any problem will simply cure itself. There are admittedly some instances in which a bad tank of gasoline, for instance, will cause ir-regular behavior, but these are rare. When you feel the car jerking, or the brakes seem strange, or the car won't make it uphill, don't hope for the car to perform its own repair. Take your car to a competent mechanic who will find out why you are hearing that unusual noise or feeling that strange symptom.

Caring for Your Car Is
Your Responsibility

For a while there was a very popular option available on some cars. It provided a prerecorded voice that would remind drivers that they had left the key in the ignition or a door ajar. The voice was a human sounding voice (in either a female or male version) which almost made you feel that there was a little man or woman hidden under the dash, watching your every move. Perhaps the Big Brother feeling made those vocal reminders lose popularity. But let's suppose for a moment that your car was equipped with a little black box that could actually advise you—or a prospective buyer —how well you have cared for your car. Might your car say: "My oil and filter have not been replaced in 10,000 miles"? How would you feel about the voice telling you that you haven't checked the tire wear or air pressure for over a year? Suppose this little voice in the dash told your passengers that your brakes haven't been checked in years, or a clogged air filter is wasting gasoline and causing air-polluting, dirty tail-pipe emissions? Most drivers give lip service to the great care they give their cars, but in your case is it really true that you care for your car as well as you should?

Let's start with checking the motor oil. It is a simple chore that requires nothing more than a clean paper towel and knowing how to open the hood and read the oil dipstick. Yet all too many car owners never ever check their motor-oil level between oil changes. If there are no leaks there is no problem. But if even a slight leak develops, eventually the motor-oil level will drop to a point where the engine is starved for oil. Allowing an oil leak to go unrepaired would be like allowing an open wound on your body to bleed. When the leak continues to where the oil is below a specific level, premature engine-bearing wear takes place: Without enough oil, the bearings heat up and, in a very short period of time, melt—destroying the engine. The oil pressure light is not intended to remind you to check the oil level. It will tip you off to a low oil level, but it may be too late. To live a long life, your engine must have enough oil to function properly. It is part of your job as the driver of a car either to check your own oil regularly or to be sure it is correctly checked whenever you refill your fuel tank.

Where is the logic in paying, on average, $16,000 for a car, and then trying to save money by putting off needed repairs?

Over the years dealing with car owners I have known many, particularly those experiencing economic hard times, who will jeopardize the life of their car to save money. For example, let's consider repeated hard starting on cold mornings. If it suddenly becomes difficult to start your car there has to be a reason. Hard starting on a cold morning might, on modern fuel-injected cars, be nothing more than a defective engine-coolant temperature sensor. A coolant sensor could be diagnosed and replaced for less than a hundred dollars. Ignoring the problem in the hopes that it will cure itself risks damage to the starter, premature battery failure, and gasoline contamination of the motor oil, along with the premature piston-ring and bearing wear it will cause. And you may contribute to the demise of your costly catalytic converter. Your car can't repair itself. A car won't grow a new muffler. You, as the owner, have to become interested in noticeable changes and make sure they are corrected. You have to be keenly aware of any sudden change in the normal operation that would indicate repairs are needed.

There is more to good car care than changing the oil and filter. Frequent oil and filter changes, using the best quality motor oil and oil filter, are your best protection against premature engine failure. You have a greater responsibility if you want your car to last longer. Don't rely solely on your car dealer or mechanic to suggest needed services like automatic-transmission fluid and filter changes. Check the owner's manual to find out when to have specific services done. Keep detailed records. When it comes to automatic-transmission fluid and filters, generally car makers will recommend that a car used in heavy-duty service will require more frequent transmission fluid and filter changes. City driving would be considered heavy-duty use simply because a transmission works harder in stop-and-go city driving. If you fail to follow the manufacturer's suggested interval for transmission fluid and filter service, you risk premature transmission failure, which could cost from a few hundred to a few thousand dollars to repair. If you drive in the city, my recommendation is to change the transmission fluid and filter every 25,000 miles.

I have known car owners who spent $300 or more to repair the air conditioners on cars with nearly bald tires and in desperate need of a wheel alignment or major engine repairs. A major part of keeping your car running reliably is developing priorities. If your car needs an air conditioner repair and a set of tires, the tires should be the top priority. Before you buy new tires find out why you needed them in the first place. If the wheel alignment is not within specification the tires will wear prematurely and that wastes money. While you're grinding rubber off the tires unnecessarily, you will also be wasting power and gasoline, pushing the car against the increased rolling resistance that misalignment causes. Take the opportunity, while the tires are being replaced, to have the brakes checked. Allowing worn brake pads to score the brake rotors could turn a $50 repair into a $250 one simply because you waited too long. Check your tire air pressure and the tire treads for signs of premature wear once a month.

Sweat dripping down your back on a hot summer may send marching orders to the brain that repairing the air conditioner be your top priority. But if that little voice under the dash could really think, it would warn you that faulty ignition wires are causing a gas wasting engine misfire and hard starting in damp weather. Your car will never break down if the air conditioner isn't cold, but bad ignition wires could keep your car from starting. Keeping faith with your car requires that you not assume that changing the spark plugs and the air filter is all there is to a tuneup.

When a tuneup is recommended by your owner's manual or because you are experiencing symptoms of loss of power, stalling, high fuel consumption, or misfire, what you mean by the word tuneup must be fully understood by you and your mechanic. It is not enough simply to order a "tuneup" because to some mechanics and car owners that may mean only changing the spark plugs and possibly checking the engine timing. To others it may mean also checking the ignition system with an oscilloscope. But to be effective, a tuneup should mean that the spark plugs, fuel filter, air filter, breather, and pcv valve are replaced as needed; the battery, alternator, starter, belts, and cooling system should be checked; and, most important, it should be the time when a very thorough engine analysis is performed.

To do all of this on fuel-injected cars, particularly those with distributor less ignition systems (DIS), costly and sophisticated computerized engine-analysis equipment is required, along with the expertise to use it to its full advantage. Computerized diagnostic equipment will very quickly check compression for each cylinder, the amount of power each cylinder is contributing, the primary and secondary ignition system, fuel injection, timing, and so forth. But of all the things modern engine analyzers check for, the most important are for emission gases coming out of the tailpipe. Aside from assuring that your car will meet the tailpipe emissions standard needed to pass motor vehicle inspections in many states, these emission gases help to determine how efficiently your engine is operating. An efficiently running engine will lower tailpipe emissions and help clean up the air.

Most computerized analyzers create printed diagnostic reports with explanations any car owner can understand. Ask your mechanic to provide you with copies of the reports generated during the diagnostic part of your tuneup. The term *diagnostic tuneup* is a better way to describe what is needed to assure the most efficient performance standards on modern car engines. You should know the difference.

There is no question that your car will last as long as you take care of it. I know of hundreds of cars ten and twenty years old that are being used every day. Properly cared for, just about any car will last forever. What seems to happen is that some car owners simply neglect their cars and then moan and groan when repairs are needed. You cannot avoid repairing your car when a breakdown occurs. You can increase the likelihood of a breakdown by neglecting to do routine maintenance and by ignoring the need for a repair.

If you want your car to go on and on, you have to devote
the time and energy it takes to know what is needed to keep
the car running reliably. Develop a relationship with a good,
honest, competent mechanic, then set aside the time and
money it takes to properly care for your car. It will pay off
in reliability and extended car life, not to mention peace of
mind.

How to Save Money Caring
for Your Car

You are the proud owner of a brand new or slightly used
car. No more mass transit. No more depending on friends
for a ride. Finally, you have wheels! The last thing you want
to think about is routine car care. Yet routine car care is
what will protect your major investment in your dream machine. The need for service is inevitable. Here's how to save
money caring for your car.

For many car owners, car care is hit or miss. Sure, they
change the oil and filter when they remember. They reason,
how much service could a new car need? Months roll by
before they even consider routine maintenance. After the
second or third lubrication, they might refer to the owner's
manual and have the dealer do the routine tuneup and checking services suggested at 15,000 miles. Often they are sur-
prised at the high cost and conclude that probably much of
what was done was unnecessary. As the new-car shine fades,
their attention to service wanes. Aside from oil changes, they
wait for symptoms before bringing their car to a mechanic.
Here are some tips to help you diagnose ailments before
costly symptoms arise.

Set up a service schedule based on the recommendations
listed in your owner's manual. You might want to vary it

depending on your experience and driving needs, but don't neglect the schedule. It costs more money to deal with repairs on a crisis basis. For example, let's say you are driving a late-model imported car with front-wheel drive and most of your driving is in city traffic. You have had the oil and filter changed regularly and are nearing 30,000 miles on the odometer. The car runs and stops just fine, then suddenly one day you hear a scraping noise while braking. You wait a week or two, and then finally have the car checked. The mechanic tells you the front brake pads are worn out. In addition, you will need two new front brake rotors, at a cost of $68.80 each. You remember that when your old Chevy needed brakes, the mechanic said he could cut a new surface into the old brake rotors. This mechanic now explains that on many imported and domestic front-wheel-drive cars, the brake rotors are thinner than on your old Chevy, and cutting them could make them unsafe. So, a routine job that might have cost just $70 will now cost $207.60, simply because you waited too long to check your brakes.

Keep your tires fully inflated to prevent premature tread wear. As the weather changes, the air pressure in tires must be adjusted. Crossing the tires front to rear at regular intervals will extend tire life and provide an extra brake check. To really save money, learn how to read the tire tread. On a new tire, the tread edges are clearly defined and the tread is even all across the tire. Watch for signs of a feather-edge pattern across the tread, or a tread worn flat on one side while remaining good on the other side. Heed the warning signs. You need a wheel alignment. At the first sign of unusual tire wear or when you notice the car seems to drift to one side, have the alignment checked.

A wheel alignment will cost about $45, provided there are no worn major parts. If neglected, add the price of replacing two prematurely worn tires. That's a total cost of $300 or more. Check tire tread when you check air pressure. Be alert to handling changes that signal possible misalignment. Learn what type of alignment your car requires. Newer unitizedbody, front-wheel-drive cars, particularly smaller imports with independent rear suspensions, are more vulnerable to misalignment. Many newer cars require four-wheel alignment. Accurate alignment of all four wheels will save you costly tire wear and reduce the rolling resistance of your tires on the pavement. The result is that you save money on tires and gasoline.

The informed motorist neither neglects brake and tire inspections, nor orders unneeded wheel alignments or other services. Avoid the "just in case it is needed" approach to car repairs. If you make it your business to know what is needed, you'll profit immensely.

Shock absorbers and their first cousins, Macpherson struts, keep the tires pressed firmly against the road when braking. With worn shock absorbers, your car will rock like a boat when you stop or accelerate. You might find a loss of steering control after even a slight bump. If your wheels vibrate after a bump, you might already have a worn steering linkage or shocks. Chances are that if you notice the car doesn't seem to ride as well as it did when it was new, the shocks or Macpherson struts supplied with your car are no longer adequate to stabilize the suspension. Wheel vibration or shimmy will cause costly premature wear to the suspension and steering linkage.

Towing is a good example. Take the time to find out just how your car should be towed properly. Don't leave it up to the tow-truck driver to know or care. Many tow trucks are not properly equipped to tow cars with front-wheel drive or sports and luxury cars. On any front-wheel-drive car, incorrect installation of the J hooks, used to attach the car to the tow truck, can damage the axle rubber boots. These fragile boots protect the costly front-drive axle joints from corrosion. Replacing the axle on a Toyota, for instance, costs more than $375. Check your owner's manual for the correct towing procedure. The AAA also publishes a manual with correct towing procedures for most cars. The safest, and most costly, way to transport any car is on a flatbed truck. Next best is a wheel-lift wrecker designed to contact only the wheels of the car being towed.

Tuneup is a word so bandied about that it has lost any precise meaning. Carburetors, ignition wires, and even the distributor are fast disappearing on modern engines. On-board computers literally tune and adjust the engine as it runs. So, it is not surprising that some car owners mistakenly conclude that a tuneup is no longer needed. Spark plugs do last longer and many of the traditional tuneup items are no longer needed. However, spark plugs, air filters, PCV valves, and gas filters are still an important part of a routine tuneup. Fuel filters are often overlooked, particularly on fuel-injected cars, where they are sometimes difficult to reach. They are no less important; in fact, they are critical on fuel-injection systems.

The modern tuneup should include a computerized engine analysis that will compare the actual test results from your car with the factory standards for that make and model. In this way, a subtle defect such as a clogged fuel injector—which could cause higher emissions levels, poor power, and wasted gasoline—will be detected. Modern diagnostic techniques draw data from your car's computer and can even interface your car's computer with a central database thousands of miles from the repair shop. The tuneup should restore full power, fuel economy, and drivability, and it should ensure that your exhaust emissions meet federal and state standards.

Save repair invoices and warranty papers. File all of your repair bills and warranties at home, never in the glove compartment. Some of the better-quality brand-name brakes, master cylinders, shock absorbers, mufflers, and power-steering units have lifetime warranties. Five-year warranties are offered on batteries and ignition-wire sets. One-year warranties are given for some remanufactured engines, alternators, and starters. The catch is that no warranty papers and no invoice means no refund. Use the invoices to refer back and check on things such as whether you have changed the transmission fluid and filter as recommended or when you had the last tuneup. Make sure the repair shop clearly describes the repair and the mileage on every invoice.

Not every transmission failure requires an overhaul. Transmission-seal leaks can be repaired for a fraction of what it would cost to overhaul the transmission. If neglected, a leaking transmission seal causes a loss of transmission fluid, which can eventually lead to serious transmission damage. Watch for leaks and be alert to changes in the way the transmission shifts. A simple adjustment will often correct seemingly serious shift problems. Where possible, get a second opinion if the diagnosis suggests rebuilding the transmission.

A shattered or cracked windshield must be replaced, but when there is only a small stone chip in the glass, try having the windshield repaired. Several firms now offer a chemical that invisibly repairs damage. This process doesn't work on all damaged windshields, but at a cost of about $40, if it does work, you save the high cost of a new windshield.

Be aware of auto parts that are either inferior or counterfeit. There are look-alike spark plugs, air filters, oil filters, ignition components, and others. Even the parts boxes might duplicate or nearly match the original brand name. Prices are usually lower, but quality is seldom equal to the brand they copy. You don't save money when you pay less for a gypsy oil filter with less filtering capacity. Ask your mechanic what brands he uses, and request that, where practical, he save the old parts in the new part boxes. You'll learn the brand names and be able to check on the quality.

Gasoline quality ranges from very pure to highly contaminated. The New York State Automobile Association says you have a fifty-fifty chance of being defrauded at the gas pumps in New York State. Other states might be better, but there are numerous nationwide reports of finding everything from discarded dry-cleaning fluid to rusty water in gasoline. The owner's manual indicates the correct octane rating suggested by the car maker. Unless you're driving a high-performance car such as a Corvette, Trans Am, or Cadillac

Allanté, chances are your car will do quite well on unleaded regular. At twenty cents more per gallon, you're wasting about $3.50 for every tankful of premium if your car can use regular.

When you check the tires, look under the car for evidence of coolant leaks. Check the white-plastic coolant-recovery tank. Learn where the coolant level should be so that you will spot a sudden loss of coolant before it becomes an overheating problem. A loose radiator-hose clamp could be detected and repaired for about $15 or less. If neglected, the loss of coolant could strand you with an overheated engine. Severe overheating could damage the cylinder-head gaskets. That repair might cost $500.

Oil-filter and motor-oil changes on a regular basis are essential to prolonging the life of your engine. Inferior oils that do not meet or exceed the American Petroleum Institute (API) and Society of Automotive Engineers (SAE) ratings shown in your owner's manual are no bargain at any price. Long intervals between oil changes increase sludge, which results in costly engine wear. Change the filter when you change the oil. Check for the tell-tale signs of leaks. Red oil might indicate a transmission or power-steering leak. Greenish drips are coolant leaks. Black oil comes from the engine.

With car prices averaging more than $15,000, it pays to care for your car. You don't save money neglecting or postponing maintenance. Inevitably, you will pay a premium for failing to care for your car. Scheduled maintenance and knowing how to read the messages your car provides will make you both live happily ever after.

Fundamental Skin Care for Your Car

There are people who tell me they don't care much about the exterior of their car, just as long as the engine, transmission, brakes, and steering are in good shape. Caring for the body, or skin, of your car is just as important as changing the oil. There are several reasons why you should be concerned about how your car looks as well as how well it runs. With few exceptions, most cars are wrapped in sheet metal, which is primed and painted. In some cases there is even a clear extra coating of paint to protect the finish. Modern cars have superior resistance to rust and corrosion, but that doesn't mean you can simply ignore caring for the skin of your car. It is still a painted surface, which is really very thin. In order to protect the metal under that thin coating of paint, you have to provide regular maintenance.

Such maintenance starts with regular washing with a mild soap formulated for cars. Don't use dishwasher soap or laundry liquid to wash your car. Check your owner's manual for the recommended type of soap, cleaners, and wax for the particular finish on your car. When you wash the car, give some thought to scratches. Use a separate sponge and bucket for the roof, trunk, and hood. Wash these surfaces first. Use another sponge for the fenders and bumpers, which tend to pick up dirt and sand. If you use the same sponge first on the fenders, then on the hood, there is a good chance you will have transferred some of the dirt from the fenders to the hood. There the dirt can scratch the smooth paint finish. The minute scratches this causes will eventually break down the car's finish. Never use either sponge on the tires and wheels. Use a separate brush to avoid getting the dirt accumulated on wheels and tires into the soap and eventually onto the smooth surfaces.

It is important to wash off any contamination before it has a chance to damage your car's finish. The best protection for any car is to keep it clean and to keep it garaged. Acid rain and other impurities in the air help to damage and dull the paint finish on any car left outside in the elements. If you drive through snow and ice, you can be sure your car will have picked up either sand or salt. Wash it off the entire car and inside the wheel wells as soon as possible. While you're at it, wash off as much of the undercarriage as is possible.

Once you have the skin of your car squeaky clean and dry, apply a coat of wax. Just what type or brand has a lot to do with what the car maker specifies in the owner's manual. Don't just pick up the car polish you have had in the garage for two years and expect that it will be okay for your new car's finish. It might, in fact, be very harmful. Investigate which car waxes and polishes are compatible with the type of finish used on your car. Find out if your car has a clear-coat finish on top of the color finish. Your owner's manual has a section on protecting your car's finish. Read it before you attempt to use any cleaners, polishes, or wax. Wax your car at least twice a year, and more often if you live in an area where there is a great deal of rain or snow. Aside from making your car look better, a good coat of wax on a clean skin will help prolong the life of the car. By wax I mean the type of polish you rub on from a bottle or can. Hot wax and other treatments you get at the car wash don't hurt, but they don't come close to the protection you get with a good coat of wax. You know your car's finish is properly protected when clear water rolls off in beads. When the water just lies flat on the finish, your car needs waxing. The wax protects the finish, which in turn protects the metal. Wax and polish are inexpensive; new sheet paint or metal are not. If you neglect the surface paint, it will eventually grow dull and porous. The luster will be gone, and even a good coat of wax can't restore the shine to badly neglected paint.

Neglecting the washing and waxing generally leads to pitting, which in time leads to rust. When the rust gets a head start, it is very difficult, if not impossible, to control. The only real answer to rust is to prevent it from happening by carefully protecting your car's skin. Make no mistake: If you garage your car, it will last for an unlimited number of years without rusting or the paint fading.

Dents and scratches should be repaired promptly, especially if bare metal is showing. There is nothing that makes a car look worse than a dent that has been on the car for so long that the creases are beginning to rust. Very often the cost of repairing a dent or damage is less than you might expect. Get an estimate promptly and don't wait until the rust begins to form in the damaged area.

A clean exterior deserves a clean interior. When you are through with your weekly wash, take an extra few minutes to tidy up the inside of the car. Use a vacuum to suck up dirt tracked in on shoes. Use a damp cloth to wipe off the instrument panel and dash. There is a wide assortment of cleansers and polishes that will have the interior of your car looking brand-spanking new with just a little effort once a week.

Avoid parking in direct sun in hot weather. Sunlight tends to fade some colors. Garage your car if possible. Protect the interior with a sun screen, which will prolong the life of the dash and interior. When you drive a clean, well-waxed car, it not only looks better but makes you feel better.

Dial 800 for Help with Car Problems

In just about every owner's manual there is a section telling you what to do about your problems when your car dealer won't help. Oddly, I have found that many car owners are reluctant to call the 800 number and seek direct intervention by the car maker. Perhaps in years gone by, calling the car maker's 800 number didn't accomplish much more than waste time, but things have changed, and car makers are more eager than ever to hear your problems and solve your complaints. Insiders tell me they have finally discovered that it is generally cheaper to keep a buyer happy than to win another buyer. I heard about one study that found that one happy customer might influence eight other people to buy a product from the same manufacturer. On the other hand, an unhappy customer might influence twenty-five people against buying the product.

When you have a problem with your new car, first go directly to the dealer from whom you bought the car. If the service manager brushes you off, ask to see the owner. If he is "out of town," write him a letter and allow a week or two for an answer. If that doesn't work, call the 800 number and explain that you are getting the brush-off for what you believe is a warranty problem. Calling the car maker's hot line might take some patience, but be persistent. Be polite and don't lose your temper. Don't threaten the person at the other end; just calmly explain your problem and ask how it can be resolved. If your call brings no response in a week, call again. If a second call brings no response, try looking for the nearest zone office. Call that office and explain that you are being ignored by the customer-relations people.

In many areas there are dealership associations. You will often hear them mentioned in television commercials; or you may have to do a little digging to find them, but it can be worthwhile. You also have recourse to your local consumer-affairs offices and your state attorney general's office. In some states the bureau of motor vehicles has a complaint bureau. The more letters you write, the more pressure you put on the dealer and car maker to quickly resolve your problem.

To get the attention of the people involved, you have to have proof that you tried to resolve the problem through regular channels. Keep copies of all your letters and the invoices from the car dealer. Document everything. Make clear notes of names and titles of the people you talked to at the various factory offices. If all of this doesn't resolve your problem, write to the president of the company and briefly outline what you have been going through. At the same time, contact your local Better Business Bureau for advice on how to initiate a complaint. Ask for details about the possibility of applying for arbitration.

In my years of experience hearing and trying to resolve complaints, I have observed that very often the initial problem, such as a bad paint job or an engine oil leak, gets lost in the shuffle. The car owner becomes frustrated and becomes more interested in punishing the dealer than resolving the problem. When that happens, even reasonable attempts to repair the problem are looked at with disdain. I know it can be difficult, but try to maintain an objective, nonemotional view. Don't turn it into a vendetta against the dealer and the car maker. Remember that when you deal with some of the major automobile makers it is like dealing with the federal government. They are giant corporations, and sometimes it takes a long time to get through the bureaucracy.

There is another 800 number that you should know about. It is provided by the U.S. Department of Transportation's National Highway Traffic Safety Administration. The Auto Safety Hot Line provides a host of material to car owners at no cost. Let's say, for example, that you are concerned about a particular safety problem with your car. You might have had a friend tell you that there was a recall for brakes on your model car but you don't recall ever receiving an official notice. You can get a complete rundown of all safety recalls associated with your make and model car by simply asking for it. All you need do is call the Hot Line for a form that will provide you with a detailed computer printout of the safety defects for any make and model car you specify.

The Hot Line can also bring you a copy of a publication titled *Uniform Tire Quality Grading*. If you're in the market for tires, you should have this booklet. It lists every tire sold in the United States, along with tread wear, traction, and temperature ratings. Along with the ratings, the Hot Line will provide a pamphlet detailing what the ratings mean and how to use them when you buy tires. Child-safety seats have had their problems. You can get a report and a safety kit on child seats just by calling. There are also crash-test results, which might interest you if you are about to buy a particular new or used car. In addition, there are several other publications that might be of interest to anyone who drives a car.

You might also register any safety-related complaints you have about a car you own. The Department of Transportation puts all complaints on a computer; if and when a trend develops, the department might initiate a safety investigation. Many of these safety investigations have led to major recalls.

The number for the Auto Safety Hot Line is 800-424-9393.

Know More About Your Car

How to Select the Right Gasoline

There is a common misconception among many drivers that the higher a gasoline's octane rating, the more power they will get from their car's engine. Many drivers spend the extra money for higher-octane gasoline in the belief that it will make their little four-cylinder engine perform like a six- or even eight-cylinder engine. This is simply not true. The octane rating is a measure of the gasoline's ability to resist knock. This knock is also known as ping or detonation. It is a loud tapping sound you usually hear when the engine is warmed up and you suddenly press down hard on the gas pedal. It might come when you are going uphill or when the engine is working hard on a hot day. Knocking can be caused by poor-grade gasoline, but it can also be caused by an ignition problem, overheating, incorrect timing, or an emission-control problem. If you develop a knock, try another tankload of gasoline before you go for mechanical repairs. If knocking occurs continuously or at even the slightest acceleration, mechanical repairs should be done as soon as possible. A continuous knock can cause costly damage to the pistons and cylinder heads.

As a car grows older it is more likely to need a high-octane gasoline to control knock. Deposits accumulate in older engines and these contribute to the problem. For the most part, you should be using the octane-rated gasoline specified in your owner's manual. Some high-performance and luxury cars must have the highest octane-rated gasoline or serious engine problems will result. There are also some middle-range gasolines that have extra additives that will help clean your carburetor or fuel injectors. If you buy the higher octane for that reason, perhaps the extra cost is justified, but if you are buying high-octane gasoline for an engine designed for low octane in the mistaken impression that it will provide extra power, you are simply wasting money. Gasoline is costly enough without wasting money to buy octane you don't need. The best octane for your car is listed in your owner's manual. Unless using it causes a ping, stick with the car maker's recommendation.

Which Motor Oil Is Best for Your Car?

There are really two basic ratings for motor oil used in your passenger-car engine. The first is the API rating created by the American Petroleum Institute. The API rating is a designation of the oil grade. SF, for example, is the highest grade and can be used in all engines. Oils that are best for diesel engines have ratings of CC or CD. Generally a diesel engine will need CC, but there are some that will need a CD-rated oil. One sure way to know precisely what oil is best for your engine is to check your owner's manual. The owner's manual will specify whether you should use a CC- or CD-rated oil for a diesel engine. If your car has a gasoline engine, the owner's manual will specify a letter designation such as SF on newer cars. You can use the higher-rated SF motor oils in older engines, but never use the lower-rated oils in your newer engine.

In addition to the API letter rating, every motor oil has a Society of Automotive Engineers rating. The SAE rates the viscosity or thickness of the motor oil.

There was a time when most cars used the same grade of oil. This is not true on new cars. The advent of small, four-cylinder engines and closer working tolerances on larger engines has made the need for careful scrutiny of the precise oil grade very important. Check your owner's manual to be sure you know precisely what oil is called for under the driving conditions you encounter regularly. The same car that requires SAE 5W-30 motor oil when driven in Vermont during the winter might require SAE 10W-40 when driven in southern Texas in the summer. Check your owner's manual to know the API and the SAE rating of the oil the car maker has specified as best for your car under various driving conditions.

Ask for the correct grade of motor oil when you have your oil changed or when you add motor oil. Don't assume the mechanic will know what oil should be used. Tell the mechanic what oil you want and be sure to specify a major-quality brand. When it comes to motor oil, it is foolish to try to save money with unknown brands. The same is true of your oil filter. Find out what quality brands of oil filters are available for your car and ask for them by name. There are any number of cheap oil filters on the market that simply don't do a proper job of filtering your motor oil. You don't save money when you buy a cheap oil filter that doesn't work. You don't save money when you put off changing your motor oil and filter. Change the motor oil and filter with every change of season, more often if you drive more than twelve thousand miles per year. If your driving is in stop-and-go city traffic or in dusty areas, you may need to change the oil and oil filter more often. A good clue is the condition of the air filter. If you find your air filter needs changing more frequently than once a year, decrease the mileage and time between oil changes.

Get to Know Your Tires

It always tickles me to watch a prospective new car buyer or self-styled auto expert kick the tires of a car he or she is inspecting. Although kicking the tires is something to do, it has absolutely no use in checking a car, nor, in particular, checking a tire. The only valid way to check a tire is to get close to the tread. This means that you either get down on your hands and knees in the driveway or have the car put up on a lift in an auto-repair facility. I prefer the second method because it allows you a better overall view of the tire, and it is much easier on your knees.

The first thing you should look for when checking a tire is the depth of the tread. The tread is the fancy grooved pattern molded into the tire. The tread has a very important function: It helps the tire grip the road surface. On a smooth, dry road, the tread is not very important. Take as an example the smooth tires used on Indy race cars. These "racing slicks" work well on smooth, dry pavement, but when even just a little moisture accumulates on the surface, the slick tires lose their grip on the road. When the tires on your car wear thin, to the point where the tread is nearly gone, your tires act like racing slicks and no longer grip the road. On a turn or in a panic stop, even on dry pavement you could lose control. In rain, ice, or snow, a worn tire with little or no tread is extremely dangerous.

The best way to learn to recognize a tire with worn tread is to compare the tread depth on a brand-new tire, possibly your spare, with the tread depth of the tires on your car. If your spare is old, stop in a tire store and examine a new tire. You will see that each of the grooves between the treads is roughly a quarter of an inch deep. Compare that depth to the tread depth on your tires. You can use a tread-depth gauge or a ruler. One good rule of thumb is to use a Lincoln-head penny. Insert the penny into the tread head first. If you can see Lincoln's forehead, your tires are worn to a point where they should be replaced.

It is possible that when you inspect your tires you will find that the tread on one side of the tire is worn thin, whereas on the other side it is quite deep. This uneven tire wear is an indication of a steering or suspension problem. Wheel alignment, worn suspension parts, or an improper wheel balance could be the culprit. Replace the worn tire, but have the cause of the problem corrected before you damage the new tire.

When choosing a tire, there is a great deal more to know than the size. For example, let's say your tire is marked, in the P-metric scale, *P195/75R14*. The *P* means the tire is for use on a passenger car. The *195* describes the width of the tire in millimeters at the widest point between the sidewalls. The *75* describes the aspect ratio between the tire height and its width; a tire with a lower aspect ratio is wider and lower and will provide quicker steering. The *R* means the tire is of radial construction, as opposed to the older bias-belted construction used before radial tires were developed. The number *14* describes the diameter of the wheel in inches. Never try putting a fifteen-inch tire on a fourteen-inch wheel—it just won't work.

The size of a new tire must be the same as the tire you take off the car, unless you are changing all four tires. In that event you can change P-metric sizes within certain limits. Consult a tire expert before you change tire sizes.

In addition to the P-metric markings on the tire, there are some other important figures that will help you determine how good the tire you plan to buy really is. There are ratings for the tire's resistance to heat. This is the temperature rating. There is also a grading for traction or straight-line stopping ability on wet pavement. A tire with an *A* rating for temperature or traction is a better tire than one with a *B* or *C* rating. Tread wear is also shown in the form of a number, such as *200* or *300*. The higher the tread-wear number, the longer the tire will last. Although a tire with a very high tread-wear rating will last longer, it might also provide a harder ride. It is a good idea to know what the ratings mean and then ask your tire dealer to explain the differences. As an example, the B.F. Goodrich Comp TA tire is an outstanding tire, with an *A* rating for traction and temperature and a tread-wear grade of *340*. Yet it costs more than a Cordovan Grand Prix Touring ST tire with a tread-wear rating of 420.

If this isn't confusing enough, try understanding tire speed ratings. Some high-performance tires, such as those used on, for example, a Corvette, have speed ratings. An *S* marked on the tire indicates a top speed of 112 mph; *H* means the tire will take speeds up to 130 mph; *V* means it will handle 149 mph; and a *Z*-rated tire will safely handle speeds in excess of 149 mph. The point is that you must do some homework before you buy new tires. Ask about speed, traction, temperature, and wear ratings. Also learn how the tire is designed. Will it handle well in the rain or is it a dry-pavement tire. Is it an all-season tire, which will do well in rain and snow as well as on hot, dry pavement? Most important of all, don't choose the tire solely on price. A cheap tire will probably not provide the safety margin a slightly higher-priced tire will afford. When it comes to tires, you probably can't afford cheap tires.

Make checking your tires a routine part of your car-maintenance regime. Check the air pressure at least once a month and before any major trip. Air pressure is a vital factor in preventing premature tire wear and failure. Tires with low pressure burn more gasoline, wear faster, and run hotter. The air pressure in your tire changes with the outside temperature. When you do your monthly air-pressure check, check the tread depth and look over the tire for uneven wear. Any bulge or bump in the tire surface is cause for concern.

If you would like more detailed information about tires, call the U.S. government's Auto Safety Hot Line. They will provide a free list of all tire ratings. You can also obtain an informative free booklet about tires by sending a stamped, self-addressed envelope to *New Consumer Tire Guide*, Box 1801, Washington, D.C. 20013.

About Suspension Systems

If you have ever ridden a bicycle, you know that every bump in the road is transmitted through the rear seat and right to your rear end. This occurs because there is a direct solid connection between the rear wheel and the frame of the bicycle. Every hole allows the tire to drop and every bump makes it move upward suddenly. To make your car ride comfortably and glide smoothly over the bumps and holes in any road, a suspension system of one type or another is used. Essentially, what the suspension system does is create a flexible connection between the wheels and the rest of the car. On most cars the front wheels are suspended in such a way that they move up and down independently. For this up-and-down movement to occur, each of the front wheels is attached to a linkage. The linkage keeps the wheel attached to the car but allows it to move up and down. The weight of the car rests on a spring, generally a coil spring. In some vehicles the spring is not a coil of steel but rather flat lengths of steel bound together and known as a leaf spring.

When you hit a small bump in the road, the front wheels bounce up and over the bump while the car stays relatively level. The spring compresses to absorb the impact of the tire and wheel against the bump. When you have passed over the bump, the spring extends once again. Left by itself the spring would continue to vibrate, allowing the car to react to the bump by bouncing up and down as it travels down the road. A shock absorber or Macpherson strut is used to dampen the vibrations of the spring and stabilize it after you hit a bump or hole. Shock absorbers also help keep the tires from bouncing off the road in reaction to bumps, braking, and on turns. Shock absorbers are an important and often overlooked part of the suspension system.

There are two basic front-suspension designs. Both include ball joints, which are really ball-in-socket devices used to allow the suspension to be flexible. Ball joints are a critical part of any suspension system. They must be lubricated and inspected for wear regularly. A worn ball joint can come apart, causing the suspension system to collapse and your car to break down.

Rear-suspension systems also vary with the type of car. Some are very simple, such as those used on rear-wheel-drive cars. Others, such as those on front-wheel-drive cars whose rear wheels are independently suspended, are far more complicated. Regardless of which system is used on your car, it is essential that the wear points such as ball joints and control-arm and strut-rod bushings be checked often. These items take a tremendous beating and can wear without your knowledge during normal driving. Make having your steering and suspension systems checked regularly a routine part of your maintenance schedule. The condition and precise wheel-alignment angles of the component parts of your suspension system are important to good maintenance. Neglecting a needed wheel alignment can result in premature tire wear, wear to steering and suspension parts, reduced gas mileage, poor handling, and overall unnecessary wear and tear on your car.

The Importance of Engine Power Balance

When an internal combustion engine runs, there are a great many things going on at the same time. The crankshaft is turning, the camshaft is turning, the timing belt or chain is spinning, and the pistons are racing up and down in each cylinder. The valves are rapidly opening and closing at just the right time to ignite the fuel-and-air mixture that will create the explosions that power the engine. When it all works together, the engine runs smoothly and might even seem to be purring. When all of the systems are working properly, they are in balance. When they are not, the engine is out of balance, and you notice it as a rough idle and poor power.

Your first instinct, when your engine doesn't seem to have the power it should, stalls, or is difficult to start, might be to simply ask your mechanic for a tuneup. If the problem were caused by worn-out spark plugs, a tuneup might correct the problem. However, changing spark plugs for any of these symptoms is a gamble. You might be correct or you might be throwing money away. The smart way is to have the engine tested to find out the cause of the problem. On modern engines, particularly those with fuel injection and distributorless ignition systems, the only real way to check for defects is with a computerized engine analyzer.

Computer engine analyzers are incredibly complicated machines that use special computer programs to run your engine through literally hundreds of tests in a very short time. Modern engines are so complicated that even the best mechanics have difficulty in remembering all that needs to be performed and how to do the checking. This is where the beauty of a computer engine analysis comes in.

The oscilloscope test is a very basic part of any engine analysis. Basically the "scope" test, as mechanics like to call it, provides the mechanic with a visual picture of the ignition system. If a spark plug is misfiring or an ignition wire has shorted, a good mechanic will see this on the scope pattern. Simply changing spark plugs when the problem is caused by a shorted ignition wire would not cure the problem. The ignition wire or an entire set of wires would have to be replaced. If the shorted wire is replaced, the scope pattern will immediately reflect the repair.

However, supposing a mechanic does a scope test and finds the ignition system—including the spark plugs, ignition wires, distributor cap and rotor, ignition coil, and so on—in good condition, yet the engine still has poor power and a rough idle. Here is where the cylinder power balance becomes important. Theoretically, every cylinder should contribute the same amount of power to run the engine. So, if you have an eight-cylinder engine and you disable one of the cylinders, you have taken away an eighth of the power of the engine. Let's say your engine normally idles at 650 rpm. If you were to disconnect the spark-plug wire on one of the cylinders, the engine idle speed might slow down to 600 rpm. This slowing down should occur in the same way for each of the cylinders. It stands to reason that if disabling the number-one cylinder reduces the idle speed by 50 rpm, disabling any one of the other cylinders should reduce the idle by the same amount; that is, provided the cylinders are working properly before you disabled them.

The idea of the cylinder power-balance test is to disable one cylinder at a time to see if each one causes the same reduction in engine rpm. If any one of the cylinders causes no reduction or very little reduction in engine rpm when it is disabled, there is something wrong in that cylinder. This is a test mechanics have been doing for years to pick out a cylinder that isn't working properly. In the old days, they did the test by individually shorting out each of the spark plugs or simply removing the ignition wire from each individual spark plug one at a time. A good mechanic could hear the change in the engine sound as he disconnected the spark-plug wire. Modern engines are more complicated and really require the technology of a computerized cylinder power-balance test.

What occurs during this test is that the computer engine analyzer determines just when the spark plug for each cylinder is about to be fired. It then shorts out the ignition momentarily so that there is no spark delivered to that cylinder at the moment the spark is needed to ignite the air-fuel mixture in the cylinder. This is done automatically for each cylinder. The results are then displayed to the mechanic on the computer screen. This very accurate test points the mechanic to any cylinder that is not contributing its full share of the power. Where the test indicates a cylinder that does not cause a lowering of engine rpm when it is shorted, there is trouble in that cylinder. The trouble could be bad piston rings, worn valves, worn cylinder heads, a blown head gasket, or an ignition problem. Wherever there is a lowering of cylinder efficiency, the cylinder power-balance test points to the problem. It is up to the mechanic to determine precisely what is causing the loss of power in the individual cylinder.

Another important feature of a computerized engine analysis is an electronic compression test of the engine. This is done very quickly by measuring the amount of electrical current the starter is drawing at the moment of the compression stroke for each of the cylinders. A mechanic can't really do this without the aid of a computer engine analyzer. It takes the computer program to record the starter amperage draw at the precise moment that both the intake and exhaust valves are closed and the starter is cranking the engine. The theory is that it will take more electrical current to turn the starter during the compression stroke than it does during the time when either the intake or exhaust valves are open and the pressure in the cylinder is lower. A cylinder with low compression requires less effort by the starter to turn the engine during the compression stroke for that cylinder. A cylinder with low compression might have bad valves, worn piston rings, or some other mechanical problem. An engine

that shows a variation in the amount of current it takes for
the starter to turn the engine points the mechanic to a cylinder
with low compression.

   The point is that simply changing spark plugs and assuming
the problem is corrected is foolish. Whenever there is a problem of rough idling, poor power, or an obvious misfire, a
computerized engine analysis should be performed to determine engine balance. If there is a worn valve or bad pistons
that are lowering the compression, all the spark plugs and
oil additives in the world are not going to make an iota of
difference. Nothing can repair a burnt engine valve but a new
valve. Nothing can repair worn piston rings but new piston
rings.

   Modern computer engine analyzers have many more capabilities. They offer tests that will reveal a fuel-delivery
problem that might be caused by a clogged fuel injector, bad
carburetor, or intake-manifold gasket leak. One of the great
achievements of modern engine testing is that a printed diagnostic report is now available. This report provides the car
owner with a record of the tests, and on the better machines
it offers diagnostic conclusions about what needs to be done
to correct the problem. The only way you can really be sure
that your engine is running up to its full potential is to have
a complete, computerized engine analysis done whenever you
suspect trouble or when a tuneup is performed. The engine
should come out with a good report at the end of the test.
All cylinders should be working, and the exhaust emissions
should be within specifications. You don't want to pollute
the air, nor do you want to waste fuel. In those states where
exhaust emissions are checked as part of the state motor-
vehicle inspection, a computerized engine analysis, including
a check of exhaust emission gases, should be done as part of
your tuneup.

   This type of testing is expensive, so don't compare this
type of diagnostic tuneup with simply installing new spark
plugs. There is a vast difference between a diagnostic tuneup
performed on a computerized engine analyzer by a competent

mechanic and one where a mechanic simply checks spark plugs and possibly the timing. Don't be taken in by a low price. Be sure you are getting a diagnostic tuneup, which includes the tests I have mentioned. Anything less is a waste of money.

Inside the Ignition System

You insert the ignition key and in a moment the powerful internal combustion engine under the hood of your car roars to life. The entire process starts with the electric starter doing what motorists once did by hand. The starter cranks the engine, or causes the crankshaft to rotate. The movement of the crankshaft sets the pistons and valves in motion. This mechanical movement creates a vacuum, which causes the mixture of fuel and air to be drawn into the cylinders. The air-and-fuel mix is then compressed in the cylinders during the compression stroke of the piston.

Here is where the ignition system comes into play. The precise mixture of air and fuel is compressed under high pressure in the tiny space left when the piston reaches the top of the cylinder. The intake and exhaust valves are closed. At just the precise moment the spark plug—inside the combustion-chamber section of the cylinder, formed by the piston, cylinder walls, and cylinder head—fires an electric spark across its electrode tip. This spark ignites the compressed air-fuel mixture. A violent explosion occurs, creating a massive pressure on the top of the piston. The piston moves downward in the cylinder, putting pressure on the crankshaft to rotate. That downward movement of the piston transmits the power of the explosion to the crankshaft and, in turn, to the transmission and driving wheels.

When and how that spark occurs is the function of the
ignition system. The high-voltage spark is created in the ignition coil when the 12-volt electrical current is suddenly
switched off. On very old cars, the spark occurred when the
contact points in the distributor were momentarily opened.
The contact points were opened by a tiny cam in the distributor, arranged in such a way that the points would open at
just the same moment in which the air-fuel mix in the cylinder
was ready to be ignited. At the same time, the distributor
rotor directed the high-voltage electrical current from the
coil to the correct spark-plug wire. Each of the spark-plug
wires was plugged into the distributor cap. The rotor spun
around in the cap distributor, directing a spark to each spark-
plug wire at precisely the correct moment.

In more recent ignition systems, the points have been completely eliminated and the spark is controlled by a transis-
torized electronic-ignition system. The basic concept is the
same, but instead of having a mechanical switch, where the
points open and close rapidly, the switching is done by a
solid-state transistor, which does not wear out like points and
can operate at a higher speed. A small iron wheel spins near
the electronic switch device and switches the coil on and off
as needed to create the spark. In that there is no mechanical
contact, there is little wear.

The modern electronic-ignition system still incorporates
the distributor, with the distributor rotor spinning around
just under the distributor cap and sending a spark to each of
the spark-plug wires.

As efficient as modern electronic ignition is, it is already
obsolete. The system of choice eliminates the distributor
completely. A spark is still created by momentarily switching
off the 12-volt electrical current to an ignition coil, but on
modern systems the coil is controlled by a powerful computer.
Instead of just one coil, there might be a coil for every two
cylinders or even one coil for each cylinder. This system
eliminates the need for a distributor, hence the term distributorless ignition system (DIS).

Be it the old-fashioned contact-point system, a modern electronic-ignition system, or the state-of-the-art distributor-less ignition system, the purpose is the same: to send a spark to the spark plugs at just the precise moment to provide maximum engine efficiency. A moment too late or a moment too soon and the engine will run poorly, burn too much gas, lose power, or not run at all. The ignition system starts with the 12-volt electrical current supplied by the battery and eventually the alternator. It runs through the ignition-key switch to the coil, the distributor switching system, and on to the high-voltage ignition wires and finally the spark plugs. On modern computerized cars, the ignition system might be controlled by the onboard computer located under the dash or in the engine compartment. As its name implies, the ignition system ignites. What it ignites is the compressed fuel-and-air mix in each cylinder at the moment the intake and exhaust valves are closed and the piston is at the top of the cylinder.

Fuel Injection Versus the Carburetor

Ever since the earliest days of automobiles, the carburetor, in various forms, has been the system of choice for mixing gasoline and air for use in the internal combustion engine. Really primitive carburetors used a rotating wire brush to change the liquid gasoline into little droplets that would vaporize as they were mixed with incoming air. As technology improved, the carburetor venturi was introduced, providing a practical system for precisely mixing the air and fuel. The design of a carburetor throat or venturi causes the rush of air through it to create a low-pressure area. Liquid gasoline pumped to the carburetor reservoir is drawn up through a metered tube protruding into the flow of air. As the liquid gasoline exits the tube it forms droplets, which soon become gasoline vapor.

The more air rushing through the carburetor venturi, the more fuel is drawn up the tube. The precise mixture of air and fuel is critical to the proper operation of an engine. Too much fuel makes a mixture difficult to ignite and burn. It results in wasted gasoline, black smoke from the tailpipe, spark-plug fouling and loss of power, high exhaust emissions, and possible damage to the catalytic converter. A mixture that has too much gasoline in relation to air is known as a rich mixture. Where the carburetor does not provide enough fuel to form the correct fuel-to-air ratio, the result might be a loss of power, hard starting, high exhaust emissions, stalling, and misfire or bucking. When there is not enough fuel in relation to the amount of air, the condition is known as lean mixture, which causes the same types of problems.

Over the years the traditional one-barrel carburetor—that is, a carburetor with one venturi or throat—has given way to carburetors with two or four venturi, also known as a four barrel. Some high-performance engines have as many as four carburetors. Carburetors have gone from very simple devices to highly sophisticated machines with all sorts of levers, passages, metering valves, pull-offs, and complex adjustments. The automatic choke is used on carburetors to provide extra fuel for starting a cold engine. Electronic carburetors have mixture-control solenoids that further control the flow of fuel. As they have become more complicated, carburetors have become more expensive to build and far more difficult to adjust and repair. This is a major reason why most modern cars are going the way of fuel-injection systems. The fuel-and-air mixture can be more precisely controlled on a fuel-injected engine than it can be through a carburetor. Carburetors can be made to work very efficiently at a precise speed under precise conditions. It is their ability to adapt to constant changes in load, temperature, and speed that make fuel-injection systems far superior to carburetor systems.

There are different variations of fuel injection, which are

too complicated to go into here but essentially they all work the same. Fuel injection squirts the gasoline directly into the intake manifold. It does not depend on the rush of air, as does the carburetor, to suck fuel into the engine. Small valves known as fuel injectors are arranged either at each cylinder or at the mouth of the intake manifold. At the precise moment, the fuel-injector valve pulses open for a moment, spraying gasoline into the air that has been drawn into the intake manifold by the action of the pistons. The amount of fuel spraying into the manifold during each pulse of the injector can be controlled by the time the fuel-injector valve is kept open. This time is called the pulse width. The longer the injector is kept open, the wider the pulse width, the more fuel is squirted into the manifold, the richer the mixture. The shorter the injector is open, the less fuel is injected or squirted into the manifold, the narrower the pulse width, and the leaner the fuel mixture.

The exciting thing about fuel injection is that the amount of fuel the injector sprays out at any given moment can be very accurately controlled. It is for this reason that you do not need to step on the gas pedal when starting most fuel-injected cars; carburetor counterparts require you to pump the gas pedal once or twice to prime the engine with gasoline. There is no automatic choke needed on a fuel-injected engine; the amount of fuel is controlled by the onboard computer. The computer senses the amount of fuel needed, depending on the temperature, load, and speed, and instantly adjusts the flow. On a cold engine, instead of the choke closing as it would on a carburetor, the computer senses the engine is cold and simply widens the pulse width to send more fuel to start the cold engine. With fuel injection, the changes are instantaneous; there is no warmup and there is no waste of fuel, as there is when the automatic choke dumps extra fuel into the intake manifold. On fuel-injection systems the flow of fuel can be stopped completely in an instant if the computer decides, for example, that the engine is flooded. This would be impossible with a carburetor.

Think of a fuel-injection system as a very precise system of fuel valves spraying only the amount of fuel that is needed, just where it is needed, in the precise amounts, for only so long as it is actually needed. Fuel injection is to the carburetor what the electric refrigerator is to a block icebox. The modern fuel-injection system is truly incredible in its ability to adapt to changing circumstances and to precisely control the air-fuel mixture. Without this electronic miracle, the low emissions and high gas-mileage standards now required by federal and state regulations would be difficult if not impossible to meet.

Respecting Your Automatic Transmission

The automatic transmission on your car is actually an incredible device that is second only to the electric starter in making it possible for just about anyone, even people with major physical disabilities, to easily drive a car or truck. Before automatic transmissions became available on production vehicles, the standard or manual transmission was what everyone drove, even on the most expensive luxury cars. There were several attempts at semiautomatic transmissions and early electrically controlled transmissions, but they never really caught on. The introduction of fully automatic hydraulic transmission truly changed the way the world drove.

Essentially an automatic transmission does what a standard or manual transmission does, but without any effort on the part of the driver. The foot-operated clutch that so many drivers have trouble operating is the coupling between the manual transmission and the engine. On an automatic transmission this connection is made with a device called a torque converter. If you don't depress the clutch when a manual transmission is in gear and you bring the car to a stop, you will stall the engine. On an automatic, the torque converter does this for you.

To understand how a torque converter operates, think of two electric fans facing each other. When one fan is turned on it blows air into the second fan, causing it to turn without being plugged into an electric outlet. On an automatic transmission's torque converter, the front part of the torque converter is rotated by the engine. It forces hydraulic fluid instead of air against the fanlike vanes of the back section, which is connected to the main transmission shaft.

The gear changes that the driver would make on a standard transmission using the shift lever and clutch occur automatically through a complex system of valves and fluid passages. The valves apply and release hydraulic pressure to servo-mechanisms, which turn a variety of clutches on and off. These clutches control the various parts of the heart of the transmission, a device called a planetary gear system. If you are interested in things mechanical, take the time to find out how the planetary gear system of an automatic transmission works. It is truly fascinating, and is the secret behind the automatic transmission. It is a series of three gears that rotate around a center gear and are fitted within another larger gear. By stopping any one of these gears, the gear reduction can be changed instantly. Also within the automatic transmission are hydraulic pumps, a governor, clutches, valves, servos, and a host of incredible devices, all put together to obviate shifting by the driver and make driving a simple job.

Once you understand how complex and marvelous your automatic transmission really is, you will develop a new appreciation for driving and will not want to abuse and shorten the life of your transmission. One of the chief ways in which people ruin their automatic transmission is when trying to free the car from snow or ice. Racing the engine with the wheels slipping on ice or snow won't get you off snow or ice, and might very well overheat and damage your transmission.

A favorite pastime for some drivers stuck in snow or ice is to rapidly shift the transmission from forward to reverse in an effort to rock the car off the slippery section. It sometimes works, but at the cost of eventual transmission failure. Yet another way to overwork your transmission is to shift into forward while the car is still rolling backward. Bring the car to a full stop before you shift gears. Never, unless it is a dire emergency, try to use the transmission to stop the car. You will probably end up doing serious damage to it.

Trailer-towing has become common practice and can be done safely, provided you are careful. Don't expect to accelerate rapidly when towing a loaded trailer. It is a strain on the automatic transmission to get the extra load rolling. Accelerate slowly and keep your speed to the minimum allowable limit. Think twice about towing a heavy horse, boat, or house trailer with a small car. If you are buying a new car and intend to get a trailer, be sure to buy a trailering package. Consult with the car dealer about the capabilities of your new car to tow a trailer.

If you plan to tow a trailer regularly, consider a transmission cooler and heavy-duty radiator. Be careful about buying or renting a trailer that is too heavy for your car to tow. Information regarding your present car's capability to tow might be listed in your owner's manual, and it should be available from the customer-service department of the car maker or from the trailer or trailer-hitch supplier.

Finally, rapid acceleration and sudden stops create unnecessary wear and tear on your automatic transmission. Every time you jam the gas pedal to the floor to accelerate, you drive another little nail into your transmission's coffin. Whenever you drive your car with a transmission low on fluid, you create the possibility of serious damage. If you neglect to change the transmission fluid and filter at prescribed intervals, you risk damage to the transmission. When you push another car, allow the wheels to slip on ice or snow, or drive incorrectly, you do a little more damage. Properly treated, an automatic transmission can last for many thousands of miles. Treat it badly, and you will pay the price in costly transmission repairs sooner rather than later.

What Is a Timing Belt, Anyway?

One of the saddest things that can happen to an engine is that its timing belt breaks and causes costly internal damage. There are any number of engines that will partially self-destruct when the timing belt slips or breaks. For this reason, it is important to know what a timing belt is, how it works, and why it has to be replaced when there are noticeable symptoms.

Many otherwise maintenance conscious drivers never even dream of replacing the timing belt. There are really two main reasons. First, it is more than likely that their previous car never had a timing belt. Timing belts have become common on smaller engines but are rarely used on larger engines. Second, unlike an alternator belt or power-steering belt, the timing belt cannot be easily examined during a maintenance check or lubrication. The same owner might have replaced the alternator belt twice and never even thought about a timing belt. Essentially, a timing belt is made of the same material as an alternator or power-steering belt and will wear out just as they do. No belt lasts forever.

The timing belt does, as its name implies, have something to do with engine timing. It does what a timing chain does on more conventional engines. The timing belt or timing chain keeps the camshaft turning in exact synchronization with the crankshaft and distributor. If the crankshaft and camshaft are not in perfect synch, the engine will not run.

More important than the engine not running is potential damage. On some interference type engines, if the piston is coming up to the top of its cylinder at precisely the same moment the intake or exhaust valves are opening, the piston will hit the edge of the valves. This causes the valve to bend or break. When a valve bends or breaks, it can no longer close and seal off the cylinder. Even if the broken timing belt is replaced after that damage, the engine will not run properly until the cylinder head is removed and the damaged valves replaced, which is an expensive repair.

The reason a timing belt or chain slips or breaks is generally because it has simply worn out. In some cases the gear that drives a timing chain might break, but when it comes to timing belts, they are far more vulnerable to wear than are timing chains. It is important to change your timing belt at preset intervals. The timing belt on most cars should be replaced at 60,000 miles. There are exceptions, but unless the manufacturer says otherwise, it is a wise investment. On many cars with timing belts it is a simple matter to replace the water pump when the timing belt is being replaced. If you're changing the belt at 60,000 miles, consider changing the water pump at the same time.

If you are not sure whether your car has a timing belt or timing chain, check with your dealer or mechanic. There are charts available from some timing-belt manufacturers that specify the recommended intervals at which a timing belt should be changed.

Steering: One Good Turn Deserves Another

Basically there are two types of steering systems in use on modern passenger cars. The older and more traditional type, generally known as parallelogram steering, is an arrangement of a steering gear and linkage set up to move the two front wheels in response to your turning the steering wheel. Far simpler and in common use on front-wheel-drive cars, is the second type, known as rack-and-pinion steering. On the latter type, instead of an elaborate system of steering linkage, the wheels are connected to a rack-and-pinion unit, which has just two tie rods connecting it to the wheels. In addition to being simpler, the rack-and-pinion system is more compact, with fewer moving parts, and it provides a more positive steering response.

The function of the steering system is to direct the wheels in precisely the right direction in response to your turning the steering wheel. It's more complicated than it might seem because the outer wheel must turn at a different angle than the inner wheel on any turn. This means that the steering system must be designed to create that angle instantly as you turn the wheel. If both front wheels were turned at the same angle, you would have a difficult time turning the steering wheel and the car would feel extremely unstable in turns. In addition, it would cause the tires to wear very rapidly.

Older cars without power steering might be fairly easy to steer once they are rolling, but when parking, the steering is very difficult. Power steering was invented for this reason. It has made the previously difficult job of turning the steering wheel very easy—so easy, in fact, that a child of five can turn the steering wheel on just about any modern car. The system that makes the power steering work is quite complicated because it has to be a power-assist system. This means that you can still steer the car even if the power steering fails.

The power for power steering is created by a hydraulic pump, which is driven by a belt off the engine crankshaft. The hydraulic pump, known as the power-steering pump, creates a high fluid pressure on demand. When you turn the steering wheel, a system of valves—in either the steering gear on a parallelogram system or the rack-and-pinion unit valves—open to assist the steering to move in the direction you have chosen. The valves respond instantly to a change of direction or a stop in movement of the steering wheel.

There is a fail-safe system, which takes over in case a power-steering belt breaks, a hose bursts, or there is a loss of pressure for any reason. The steering wheel becomes more difficult to turn, but it can still be turned.

Any steering system is vulnerable to neglect. If you fail to have the steering tie-rod ends lubricated, they will eventually wear out and might break apart. This could result in a loss of steering because the linkage between the wheels and the steering gear or rack and pinion disconnects. Steering linkage can be damaged when you hit an obstacle in the road, in a car wash, in a collision, or as a result of improper towing. It is therefore extremely important to have the steering system carefully checked at least once a year. During an inspection of the steering system, a mechanic should look for power-steering fluid leaks, worn belts, and worn tie-rod ends. On a parallelogram steering system, the mechanic should inspect the idler arm, Pitman arm, center link, and adjusting sleeves, as well as ball joints, control-arm bushings, springs, shock absorbers, and all other components of the steering and suspension system. A worn tie-rod end or worn control-arm bushing will allow free movement in the steering and a loss of steering control. At higher speeds, this can be a dangerous condition. Even at low speeds, if there is sufficient wear in the steering linkage, the car might swerve from side to side. If there is enough wear, steering control might be lost completely. Under the right circumstances, this could cause serious injury. Worn steering linkage is a dangerous condition because the loss of steering generally comes without warning. Once the mechanic is sure the system is not worn or leaking, the final step should be to check the wheel alignment. Misaligned wheels cause premature tire wear, waste gasoline, and accelerate steering linkage and suspension wear.

If you carefully maintain your power-steering system, chances are slim that you will ever experience a total loss of power assist, but it can happen at any time. All it takes is an engine stall, a broken belt, or a loss of power-steering fluid, and suddenly you're driving a car with no power assist.

For some drivers this can be a frightening experience. If you have never driven a car without power steering, you might consider doing what airplane pilots call a dead-stick maneuver.

The dead-stick maneuver is intended to familiarize you with the feel of steering your car when the power steering and power brakes have suddenly failed. (On cars with electrically operated power brakes, you might have power braking even while the engine is not running.) Make absolutely sure there are no people or cars nearby. A deserted shopping mall where there is a large empty parking lot might be best, provided there is no chance you will tangle with another car, tree, person, or lamppost should you lose control. Check out the spot to be sure you won't hit anything if you can't steer or can't stop. Here is how it works: Drive the car in a large figure-eight pattern until you establish a course. You might want to bring along some garbage bags filled with crumpled newspaper to serve as traffic cones. Repeat your figure eights until you are comfortable driving them at ten miles per hour. Then, on the straight leg of one of the figure eights, turn off the ignition key.

CAUTION: Be careful not to turn the ignition switch to the lock position, which will lock the steering wheel; turn it one notch to off.

You will experience a sudden loss of power steering and power braking. You will still be able to steer and stop the car, but not in the same way you are used to doing. You will have to exert a much greater effort to steer, but you will discover that you can still steer the car. You will also discover that you can still stop the car, even with the engine not running. You will have to press much harder on the brake pedal, but you can still stop. The secret is not to panic and to trust the fact that you can still steer and stop when the engine dies or you lose power steering or power braking.

What Happens When You Step on the Brake Pedal

Anyone who has ever driven a car knows that when you step on the brake pedal, the car stops, but knowing just what is happening when you step on the brake pedal can give you a better understanding of how to drive safely and how to care for your brakes. By knowing how the brakes should feel, you can detect a problem in its early stages. When it comes to brakes, the earlier you detect the problem the more likely you are to save money in repairs.

When you step down on the brake pedal, you are putting pressure on a small hydraulic piston mounted in the brake master cylinder. The piston in the master cylinder acts like a pump and increases pressure on the brake fluid in the master cylinder. The master cylinder is connected to each of the wheels by a system of steel tubes and rubber hoses. At the instant you press down on the brake pedal, the brake calipers on the front wheels go into action. Reacting to the increased fluid pressure, the front brake calipers squeeze both sides of the front disc-brake rotor. To see how this works, pick up a dinner plate and grasp it with one hand. The caliper is your hand grasping the dinner plate, with the dinner plate acting as the rotor. When you step on the brake the caliper grasps the rotor very tightly until it stops turning. This stops the car. You can imagine that a steel brake rotor being grasped by a steel brake caliper would wear out quickly and make a lot of noise. For that reason, brake pads are installed between the brake rotor and the brake caliper. The brake pads are a specially designed friction material that will quickly stop the rotor and provide a maximum amount of wear.

Most modern cars have disc-brake rotors in the front and more conventional drum brakes in the rear, although a growing number of sport and luxury cars are now using disc brakes on all four wheels. The drum brake on the rear wheels also reacts to the hydraulic pressure created in the master cylinder. Instead of a caliper squeezing a brake rotor, a wheel cylinder is used. To demonstrate how drum brakes work, try picking up a coffee mug by inserting your fingers into the mug. In this case the coffee mug would act like the brake drum; your fingers would act like the brake shoes. When you step on the brake pedal, hydraulic pressure is increased in the wheel cylinders. This causes the brake shoes to move outward and contact the inside surface of the brake drum. As the pressure increases, the drum is forced to stop turning. Here again, rapid wear would take place between the steel brake shoes and the brake drum. To prevent this, a brake lining is riveted or glued onto the brake shoes. It is the brake lining or brake pad that will wear out first.

It is very difficult to know when brake pads and lining are worn thin. The best method is to have the wheels removed and the brake pads and lining physically checked. A good rule to follow with regard to the wear on front brake pads is to replace the brake pads when the friction material on the brake pad is worn to the thickness of the metal backing plate onto which it is attached. With regard to a brake lining, it is the amount of lining left above the rivet head on riveted brakes that is important. One part of the brake shoe might be fine, whereas another is worn to where the rivets are nearly flush with the brake lining. On cars where the brake lining is glued to the brake shoes, replace the lining when it is as thin as the metal part of the brake shoe. That doesn't mean, however, that it would be wrong to replace a brake lining when it is still thicker than the brake shoe. Brake linings or pads might need changing because they are loose, cracked, or nearly worn to the point of needing replacement. When you are inspecting brakes and the wear indicates new brakes will soon be needed, it sometimes makes more sense to replace the brakes rather than having to remember to have them checked in a few thousand miles and to spend the time to go through removing the wheels all over again for a reinspection.

When you understand how your brakes work, you as a driver should be sensitive to a change in the braking. If front brake pads are worn, there might be a slight pull to one side. You might feel that you have to press harder, particularly when the brakes are hot, for the car to stop. When rear brakes are worn, you will often feel the brake pedal drop lower. The brake warning light might also come on when braking. A change in the feel of the brake pedal nearly always indicates a problem. A soft pedal might indicate a loss of brake fluid. A spongy pedal could mean there is air trapped in the brake fluid. If the brake pedal seems to fade away under your foot as you wait at a stop light, you might have a defective master cylinder. If you find the brake pedal very difficult to depress, there could be a disconnected vacuum hose or a defective power brake.

When you find that the car stops but seems to roll farther before it finally stops fully, there might be a problem in the rear brakes. You as the driver should be alert to any change in the way the brakes work. When you note a change, immediately begin driving more carefully and allow greater stopping distance between you and the car ahead. Reduce your speed to a safer level and keep an eye out for the brake warning light on your instrument panel. Seek professional help as soon as possible.

One thing you can do is check the brake master cylinder for a loss of hydraulic fluid. All you need to do is learn how to remove the master-cylinder cover and check for the level of fluid. The important thing to remember is that brake fluid can damage the paint on your car. Be careful not to spill any and to wipe your hands clean after refilling the master cylinder. Using the correct brake fluid is also very important.

Brake fluid is graded DOT 3, DOT 4, or DOT 5. Most cars use amber-colored DOT 3. DOT 5 is a silicone-based brake fluid that is purple in color and is generally used in motorcycles and some high-performance vehicles. It cannot be used in place of DOT 3 or 4. Read the label twice before you attempt to add any fluid to the brake master cylinder. I have seen dozens of cases where a car owner mistakenly poured power-steering fluid, windshield-washer fluid, and even car polish into the master cylinder. The result can be very destructive to the brake system and expensive to repair.

How a Battery-Charging System Works

Aside from the mere joy of knowing how your car works, there are some good reasons for you to understand how and why the battery-charging system on your car does the job of recharging the battery. In the early days of motoring, you had to yank the crank handle to get the crankshaft moving. Once the pistons were moving up and down, the magneto fired the spark plugs and the internal combustion engine was off and running. Then along came Charles "Boss" Kettering, who changed the way internal combustion engines were started. He invented the electric starter or self-starter, as it has come to be known. From then on you didn't have to be big and burly and be able to pull the often hard-to-move crank handle to start any car or truck.

Essentially the starter is an electric motor that derives its power from the battery. When you turn the ignition switch to the start position, electrical current is supplied to a heavy switch known as a solenoid. The solenoid switch is used because the ignition switch is too small to carry the heavy electrical demand of a starter motor. As you turn the ignition switch to the start position, the current instantly engages the solenoid switch, which makes a direct electrical connection between the battery's positive terminal and the starter motor.

The starter rapidly turns a special gear, about two inches in diameter, attached to the end of the starter-motor shaft. The gear is generally called a Bendix drive. It is special in that as the starter motor gains speed, the gear also moves forward on the starter-motor shaft. The Bendix-drive gear moves forward and engages the gear teeth on the flywheel. The flywheel is essentially a larger gear about twenty-five inches in diameter. The flywheel is attached to the crankshaft. As the starter motor turns the flywheel, the crankshaft turns and the pistons, camshaft, valves, and everything else starts moving. The entire process begins just as it did when the engine was cranked by hand.

As the engine starts, the flywheel gains speed and the driver releases the ignition key. This allows the starter motor to stop spinning and the Bendix-drive gear to recede away from the flywheel gear teeth. The starter is not used again until it is needed to restart the engine.

A battery is really a chemical storage machine that stores electrical current. When you use the starter motor, you are making a withdrawal of electrical current from the battery. The starter draws a great deal more than the headlamps or radio; so, when the starter is used frequently, it takes more current to redeposit or recharge the electrical current. If a battery is not constantly recharged, it will go dead.

The heart of the charging system is the alternator. Essentially an alternator is an electrical current generator very much like a power-plant generator, only on a smaller scale. The alternator is powered by the engine through a belt driven by the crankshaft. The alternator creates alternating electrical current, which is changed to direct current by diodes within the alternator. Left on its own, the alternator would constantly charge the battery until it boiled away all of its acid and dried out. To control the electrical current or the amount of charge the alternator puts into the battery, a voltage regulator is used. The voltage regulator measures the battery charge and electrical load made by the air conditioner, heater, ignition system, radio, wipers, and so on, and adjusts the amount of charging to meet the needs of each moment. The voltage regulator might either be a part of the alternator or mounted separately. Most modern cars have the regulator mounted inside the alternator.

The system works properly when the alternator/regulator recharges the battery after each start and keeps it fully charged while the car is running. When the alternator fails to do this, the battery eventually becomes discharged and cannot start the engine.

There are some very obvious reasons why a battery goes dead. If the red alternator or charge light on the dashboard goes on, obviously the alternator is no longer recharging the battery and it is only about half an hour before the battery becomes too discharged to restart the car. But supposing the red warning light does not come on, yet you find that you have to frequently boost the battery? This can very often be the result of the alternator drive belt slipping when the alternator is charging. This reduces the power the alternator can produce and makes it possible for the battery to be less than fully charged. The same thing can happen when a voltage regulator is defective and will not allow the alternator to recharge the battery. Dirty battery terminals can also prevent proper recharging of the battery.

One of the most common causes of a battery going dead —where the charging system is in good shape—has to do with what mechanics call an electrical drain.

Drains can easily be spotted if they are caused by something such as leaving the headlights or parking lights on. It becomes more difficult when the glove compartment or trunk-light switch fails and those lights stay on. Mechanics have a test for electrical drains. Before you jump to the conclusion that you have a bad battery because it needs to be boosted, have the charging system tested. This includes a test of the electrical draw of the starter to see if it is going bad, a load test of the battery, a check of the battery terminals and cables, a test of the charging power of the alternator and regulator, a check of the alternator drive belts, and finally a careful check for electrical drain.

You should always consider the complete charging system when trying to discover why the battery has failed to start the car. If you guess, you might wind up changing the battery, alternator, or starter, only to discover in the final analysis that the problem was nothing more than a trunk light that failed to go out when you closed the trunk.

Understanding Your Car's Cooling System

It is easy to forget that within the walls of a running internal combustion engine there is a raging fire going on all the time. This fire is the rapid burning of air and gasoline inside the combustion chamber of each cylinder. The rapid burning creates the power to push each piston down and turn the crankshaft. Tremendous heat is created when each explosion occurs within the combustion chambers. Temperatures in the combustion chamber can reach 5,000° Fahrenheit. In addition, the friction created by the moving parts within the engine also creates heat. If the heat is not removed, the high temperatures will soften the metals and eventually melt them. To prevent an engine meltdown, a liquid coolant in the form of water-and-antifreeze mixture is pumped through the engine. As the coolant passes through the small passages formed in the engine walls during its manufacture, heat from the combustion chambers is absorbed by the coolant through the metal. The hot coolant is pumped through the radiator, where the heat from the coolant is transferred to the cooler air passing through the fins of the radiator. After it is cooled in the radiator, the coolant is again pumped through the engine, where it absorbs more heat.

This continuous process keeps the metal parts of the engine cool. Once there is an interruption in the flow of coolant through the cooling system, the engine rapidly overheats. The interruption can be caused by a number of things. First and foremost is a loss of coolant. When a leak occurs and coolant leaks out of the system, the heat is no longer dissipated from the hot combustion chambers. In a short time the system overheats. Adding coolant restores the system's ability to cool the engine. If the leak is not repaired, coolant will eventually leak out and the overheating will recur. Whenever there is a loss of coolant, it is not enough to simply pour more antifreeze and water into the cooling system. You must determine the cause of the coolant loss.

Normally coolant should last for years unless there is a leaking radiator, heater core, hose, core plug, water pump, or some other coolant leak. If there is a major leak, you can generally simply trace back from the accumulation of coolant on the ground to its source. If the puddle of coolant is under the radiator, chances are the radiator is leaking. If it is under the center of the car, there might be a heater hose or core plug leaking. If you can't easily see the source of the leak, you will need to have a mechanic use a cooling system pressure tester to create pressure in the system. The idea is to create the same pressure that would normally be created when the coolant is hot. The difference is that with a pressure test the coolant remains cold and there is no risk of scalding from a spurting leak of hot coolant.

CAUTION: If you learn nothing more from this book, learn this: NEVER ATTEMPT TO REMOVE THE RADIATOR CAP WHEN THE COOLANT IS HOT. If you twist off the radiator cap when the coolant is hot, it might go into a violent boil and come blasting out like a geyser.

The radiator cap is designed to control the pressure in the cooling system and keep it at about 18 psi. This helps the coolant do a better job of cooling the engine. However, it also creates a condition in which the coolant will go into a boil when it is hot and the radiator cap is removed. A leak in the cooling system that allows a pressure loss will also cause the coolant to boil at a temperature where it would not boil were it still under pressure. That may seem complicated, but it is important to keep the cooling system free of leaks, which will result in a loss of coolant and a loss of pressure.

For the cooling system to transfer heat from the engine to the outside air, the water pump must keep turning. If a fan belt breaks, the water pump no longer turns. The coolant is no longer pumped through the engine and the radiator, and the result is overheating. This is another good reason to frequently check fan belts. A worn belt can break, which will cause the water pump to stop turning. On most rear-engine cars, the radiator fan is turned by the water pump. When the pump stops, the fan stops and the engine overheats. On most front-wheel-drive cars, the fan is turned by an electric motor mounted on the radiator. If the electric fan does not go on when the radiator is hot, the coolant will not be cooled and the engine will overheat.

I have saved the thermostat for last because it is probably the most misunderstood part of the cooling system. The thermostat is a valve in the cooling system that keeps the coolant from flowing to the radiator until the engine has reached its normal operating temperature of about 195° Fahrenheit. When you first start your engine, the thermostat is closed. As the temperature of the coolant rises rapidly, the thermostat begins to open and allow the hot coolant to circulate through the radiator. If the thermostat fails to open, the coolant just gets hotter and hotter and eventually the engine overheats. Well, you might ask, why not simply remove the thermostat entirely? In an emergency you can do that. However, the thermostat is an important part of the cooling system and is needed, winter and summer, to control the engine temperature. When an engine is too hot, it will overheat. When it is not hot enough, it will function poorly and that will create high pollution, high fuel consumption, low power, and poor performance. When the thermostat does not open, the engine will probably make a banging noise and boil over.

It is important to maintain your cooling system so that it will not become contaminated and rusty. Rust and corrosion in the cooling system result from a breakdown of the rust inhibitors in the coolant. When the corrosion or rust becomes severe, the tiny passages in the radiator begin to block up, and the passages in the heater core and the engine block and cylinder heads become clogged. The clogging restricts the flow of coolant. Restricted coolant flow causes overheating. Check the color of the coolant frequently. If it is turning a rust color, you probably already have a clogged cooling system. There are any number of chemicals that can be used to clean and unclog your cooling system. If nothing else works, the radiator might have to be removed and cleaned. Careful attention to the cooling system will save you money by preventing rust and corrosion, along with the costly breakdowns they cause.

About Air Conditioners

"My air conditioner works fine but it blows hot air." Obviously, if it blows hot air it isn't working fine at all. What makes an air conditioner cool your car is its ability to circulate cool air through your car. Here is how it works. Refrigerant gas has a very special quality: It will boil with very little heat. Just like water boils on a stove, refrigerant gas under pressure will boil only at a far lower temperature.

When water boils on a stove it absorbs the heat from the fire under the pot. In an air conditioner the refrigerant gas actually boils or vaporizes in the air-conditioner evaporator located under the dash. Air from the passenger compartment is blown across the coils of the evaporator, which looks sort of like a little radiator. As the refrigerant gas boils in the evaporator, it absorbs heat from the air passing through the coils. This transfer of heat and moisture from the passenger-compartment air is what cools the air and eventually you. The air then circulates through the passenger compartment to pick up more heat.

In order to get the refrigerant gas to boil or vaporize efficiently it has to be pumped up to a high pressure. Refrigerant gas becomes a liquid when it is cooled under high pressure. The air-conditioner compressor pumps the gas in the system up to a high pressure. It then passes through a device located in front of the radiator called the condenser. In the condenser the hot refrigerant gas under pressure is cooled to become a liquid. The liquid is dried and filtered, then sent to the expansion valve located at the mouth of the evaporator. On one side of the expansion valve the refrigerant is a liquid under high pressure. As the liquid passes through the expansion valve it goes from high pressure to low because the compressor has sucked the refrigerant out of the evaporator. At that moment when the liquid enters the low pressure in the evaporator it begins to boil or vaporize and absorbs tremendous quantities of heat. The vaporizing of the refrigerant cools the evaporator coils. The whole cycle is repeated over and over again to keep your air conditioner cooling.

It takes a great deal of effort to compress the refrigerant gas, and that is what the compressor does. Left on its own, the compressor might just keep pumping and cooling until either you shut off the engine or, on some systems, until it turns the evaporator into one solid block of ice. To stop the compressor from running constantly, a compressor clutch is located at the front of the compressor. A magnet pulls a plate against the surface of the clutch, causing the compressor to spin with the clutch. The whole assembly is powered by a belt off the crankshaft. When you turn off the air conditioner the electrical power to the compressor clutch is removed, the magnet releases, and the compressor stops turning. By the same token, if the system gets too cold or the pressure is too low, special switches will shut off the compressor before it self-destructs.

When the refrigerant gas of an air conditioner is lost either entirely or partially, the system will not cool as well, or not at all. Loss of refrigerant is the number-one cause of air-conditioner malfunction. Adding gas is the remedy, but it is not the cure. If the air conditioner loses refrigerant gas, a competent mechanic should use an electronic leak detector to determine the cause of the leak. It could be anything from a loose connection to a hole in the evaporator core. Either way, if the leak is not found, refrigerant gas will still be lost. This is not only costly to you as the car owner, but to the atmosphere, which is damaged when refrigerant gas escapes. Modern mechanics now use refrigerant recycling equipment to save, clean, and reinstall the same refrigerant in your car after the repair is completed.

This can be accomplished with many repairs because an air-conditioner malfunction might not always be simply a loss of refrigerant. A compressor could fail, making it impossible for the system to build up pressure. The expansion valve or accumulator filter could clog, making it impossible for the refrigerant to circulate through the system. A switch could fail, keeping the compressor clutch from engaging. It is also possible that the air conditioner is actually cooling but the cooled air is not being allowed to circulate through the car.

Air-conditioning systems are really quite ingenious and simple once you understand how they work. The danger is that you will take severe risks attempting a do-it-yourself repair without the proper safety equipment and know-how to do the job safely and properly.

> **CAUTION: Leave the recharging and repair of your car air conditioner to a competent mechanic, skilled in the proper use of recycling and protective equipment.**

Mufflers, Tailpipes, and the Exhaust System

Unless you are fortunate enough to have one of the small percentage of cars on the road today that are equipped with stainless-steel mufflers and tailpipes, you will eventually have to deal with repairs to your exhaust system. Essentially what the exhaust system does is quiet the sounds of each explosion in each of the cylinders as the engine operates. If you were to remove the exhaust system, you would hear an ear-splitting roar from the engine, which grows louder as you accelerate. If you have ever been annoyed by the loud exhaust of a two-cylinder motorcycle, you would be driven to a frenzy by a big V8 engine without a muffler. The exhaust system also transports the hot poisonous exhaust gases out to the rear of the car. In recent years, with the advent of emissions-control systems, the catalytic converter has become an integral part of the exhaust system.

The catalytic converter appears to be another muffler on the outside. On the inside, it is a complicated device that actually sets up a chemical process to reduce emissions. We generally think of automobile exhaust as being full of carbon monoxide (CO), that odorless, colorless gas that quickly kills in an unvented, confined space. In addition to CO, exhaust gases include all sorts of other nasty things, such as unburned hydrocarbons (HC), oxides of nitrogen, sulfuric acid, soot, and much more. All of these pollutants are present in the exhaust even after the electronic carburetors and electronic fuel-injection systems have done a terrific job of reducing pollution. To reduce this pollution, car makers have developed the catalytic converter. When the temperature within the catalytic converter reaches about 500° Fahrenheit, a chemical process begins that converts unburned portions of the exhaust into carbon dioxide and water. When the catalytic converter really gets warmed up, it converts nearly all of the unburned gases to a harmless exhaust. During warmup, the catalytic converter does not efficiently clean up the exhaust. It is during these first few minutes of warmup that the exhaust is the most polluting. It's another good reason to avoid prolonged warmup periods.

After the exhaust gases pass through the catalytic converter to be cleaned, they then pass through a muffler, where the sound is deadened. The catalytic converter does reduce some of the sound, but it is the special design of the muffler that really muffles or quiets the engine sounds. The length of the muffler and each of the exhaust pipes also plays its part in creating the sound. Many cars have an additional rear muffler known as a resonator, whose function it is to further quiet the sound of the engine. In future exhaust systems the sound will be deadened electronically, using speakers to duplicate the exhaust sound and play it back a fraction of a second later to cancel the actual exhaust sound we hear.

The shape and size of all exhaust components is critical. If you reduce the size of the pipes or change the size of the muffler to anything other than the originally specified design, you risk creating a back pressure on the engine that will reduce performance. When you buy a new muffler and tailpipe, be sure it is not one that is simply made to fit the pipe sizes. The muffler and tailpipe you buy for your car should meet the exacting specifications of the original car maker. This is also true of the catalytic converter. It must be designed to handle the exhaust load delivered to it by the specific engine on which it is to be used. Some catalytic converters are made with a special air tube attached, which takes fresh air from the engine's air pump. Your replacement catalytic converter should have the same air tube if it is to work like the original. A further note about catalytic converters: Because they are expensive, some car owners may opt to install just a plain pipe in place of the catalytic converter. This is an illegal practice, and should never be done. Removing the catalytic converter will increase the harmful pollutants your car pumps into the atmosphere. In those states where emissions are tested, some require that the catalytic converter be in place and working for the car to pass the state emissions test. Aside from the regulations, you breathe the air, so help keep it clean.

It is important to frequently check the exhaust system for holes, rust, and breaks. This is a check that should be made whenever the car is up on a lift for a lubrication or for any other reason. If you catch a broken muffler flange before the muffler falls out, you can save a breakdown. If you spot a broken tailpipe hanger, you might save the price of an entire exhaust system. Although it is true that your car will run perfectly well without the exhaust system, you can have a breakdown when the disconnected muffler or tailpipe wraps around the drive shaft or jams against a tire. Check your exhaust system frequently and repair it when necessary. Don't wait for the parts to fall out. When the sound of your exhaust system suddenly becomes louder, have it checked as soon as possible.

When you need exhaust repairs, use good judgment. If you need a new muffler and tailpipe, you probably need the intermediate pipe as well. Often car owners try to save money by having a new muffler and tailpipe installed on the intermediate pipe that is just as old as the muffler and tailpipe that have rusted out. Exhaust systems rust from the inside out. An intermediate pipe might look just fine on the outside but be paper-thin on the inside. If you bolt a new muffler and tailpipe to an old, rusted intermediate pipe, you might very well wind up losing the new muffler and tailpipe when the old intermediate pipe finally falls apart.

Seek out the best warranty when you replace a muffler. Generally that is a lifetime warranty on the parts. Save the warranty papers and invoice. However, don't just buy the first lifetime-warranty muffler you see. Check the prices and compare the type of muffler. Find out if the muffler and pipes are made specifically for your car and similar models, as opposed to a universal muffler that will fit many cars. Do a little shopping when you replace your exhaust system. Insist on an exact duplicate of the factory-original system, not one made to fit by the exhaust installer.

State Motor-Vehicle Inspections

Many states require a yearly motor-vehicle inspection intended to ensure that every car on the road meets a minimum safety standard. In many states that inspection includes testing of the exhaust emissions discharged from your car's tailpipe. There is an endless debate as to the merits of a required motor-vehicle inspection. There is even more debate over whether the inspections should be done by the state or by independent shops operating under the supervision of the state.

No matter who does the inspection, a thorough inspection is a good thing. The problem is that very often the inspection is only minimal or not done at all. Any motor-vehicle inspection is only as good as it is complete. The problem comes about because some car owners want to get through a motor-vehicle inspection as quickly and inexpensively as possible. This is understandable, but it defeats the noble purpose of a yearly inspection. If by hook or by crook you manage to get a motor-vehicle inspection sticker without really getting a proper inspection you are fooling no one but yourself. If you go to a place where the inspection isn't really done or not done well, you are wasting your money. The idea of a yearly motor-vehicle inspection is twofold. First, it forces those drivers who put off needed safety repairs to make their cars meet the minimum safety standards. Second, in those states where emissions testing is a part of the yearly inspection, drivers are forced to keep their vehicles from polluting the environment.

Yearly inspections are a wonderful idea when the inspections are thorough. However, you cannot assume that your car is in perfect condition and will need no further attention until the next inspection. Too many drivers see the state motor-vehicle inspection as a seal of approval that their cars need nothing more. Even if your car has passed the state inspection with flying colors, you must still keep to a strict maintenance schedule if you are to get the most out of your car.

Some drivers see the inspection laws as unfair. In fact, they help make the roads safer for you by ensuring that other cars on the road meet minimum safety standards. The thing to remember is that the standards are minimum, and are not intended as the ultimate in good car care. If you carefully maintain your car, you should have no trouble passing any state motor-vehicle inspection. If you fail to pass, it is because there is a defect that causes a safety problem or pollutes the air. Even failing an emissions test is a good thing in that it alerts you to the fact that your car is not only polluting the air you breathe but wasting gasoline—and the money you spend on it—and robbing you of power. Unsafe emissions left uncorrected could cost you extra dollars for a clogged catalytic converter. If your state has yearly motor-vehicle inspection laws, consider them an extra protection and make sure the inspection you get on your car is complete.

Plume

HOW TO WRITE—ABOUT PRACTICALLY ANYTHING

PLUME

TAKING A TRIP?

☐ **BED AND BREAKFAST 1993 by Betty Rundback.** This comprehensive guide provides a popular, affordable alternative to the mainstay of motels and hotels. "America's newest and hottest accomodations trend is Bed and Breakfast." —*Boston Globe* (269261—$14.00)

☐ **GOING TO EXTREMES by Joe McGinniss.** A vivid, often humorous account of Alaska's eccentric people and places. Recaptured is both the power and the beauty of a land still untamed and undefiled, and the endurance of a spirit of independence and adventure that finds Alaska its natural home. (263018—$10.00)

☐ **BAGHDAD WITHOUT A MAP** *And Other Misadventures in Arabia* **by Tony Horwitz.** A wild and comic tale of Middle East misadventure that reveals a fascinating world in which the ancient and modern collide. (267455—$10.00)

☐ **INNOCENTS ABROAD** *Traveling with Kids in Europe* **by Valerie Wolf Deutsch and Laura Sutherland.** You'll find practical tips to keep children from getting bored, what foods to avoid, the best times to visit famous places, and a whole treasurehouse of knowledge that parents really need to keep their dream vacation from turning into a nightmare. (265851—$15.95)

Prices slightly higher in Canada.

Buy them at your local bookstore or use this convenient coupon for ordering.

PENGUIN USA
P.O. Box 999, Dept. #17109
Bergenfield, New Jersey 07621

Please send me the books I have checked above.
I am enclosing $_____ (please add $2.00 to cover postage and handling).
Send check or money order (no cash or C.O.D.'s) or charge by Mastercard or VISA (with a $15.00 minimum). Prices and numbers are subject to change without notice.

Card # _____ Exp. Date _____
Signature _____
Name _____
Address _____
City _____ State _____ Zip Code _____

For faster service when ordering by credit card call **1-800-253-6476**

Allow a minimum of 4-6 weeks for delivery. This offer is subject to change without notice

There's an epidemic with 27 million victims. And no visible symptoms.

It's an epidemic of people who can't read.

Believe it *or* not, 27 million Americans are functionally illiterate, about one adult in five.

The solution to this problem is you... when you join the fight against illiteracy. So call the Coalition for Literacy at toll-free **1-800-228-8813** and volunteer.

Volunteer Against Illiteracy. The only degree you need is a degree of caring.